As Far As I Remember

Andrew Woodhouse

© Andrew Woodhouse, 2016

Published by Andrew Woodhouse

A CIP catalogue record for this book is available from the British Library.

ISBN 978-0-9955693-0-0

Book layout and cover design by Clare Brayshaw

Prepared and printed by:

York Publishing Services Ltd
64 Hallfield Road
Layerthorpe
York YO31 7ZQ

Tel: 01904 431213

Website: www.yps-publishing.co.uk

Acknowledgements

Many thanks to my Consulting Editor Janice Carnell for her patience and encouragement and to my fashion designer granddaughter, Agatha Daisy for the imaginative book cover.

Andrew Woodhouse.

Snowdrop

As far as I remember, I chucked the 'rotten' snowdrop into the hedge so it couldn't be seen, but I knew I was in for another beating. When you're four, it's not very funny to keep getting into bother.

Anyway, it wasn't my fault that I'd torn the seat out of the trousers of the brand new suit that had been so carefully tailored with loving care by my gran. She was an excellent seamstress and we were fortunate that this was so, because this was war time and clothes were in short supply.

She used to kit out my brother David, sister Margaret and myself and we always looked pretty reasonable even in those days of shortages, but I never really had much respect for this new addition to my wardrobe.

The suit fitted alright, but it was the colour. She'd made it from a remnant of material in a very pronounced Lincoln green. I think perhaps that was what gave me the desire to emulate Robin Hood, because when I was made to wear this nasty little two piece, I climbed up the nearest tree in the garden and perched myself on a fairly high branch (at least for a four-year-old) and awaited the Sheriff of Nottingham's men.

I'd been warned. In fact, it was more than a warning. It was a close up face to face encounter as my mother pronounced the dreadful consequences of what would happen to me if I should get so much as a speck of dirt on my new suit. Yet here I was up a tree and it seemed the whole household was searching for me. At that point, I considered it the right time to descend, a little too quickly as it happened and catching my breeches on a protruding branch, I tore them almost in two.

"Oh my God!" I called out, or at least I would've called, had I at that time of my life known of his mercy. As it was, there was no mercy and no escape standing there with shaking legs. My head was full of chastising voices and words I couldn't comprehend.

I waited for the inevitable slaps that were so very justified and always expected for crimes of this nature. It wasn't long before they rained upon my legs and caused them to glow with a pretty rosy tint.

It was a rotten suit and I didn't like it anyway. Perhaps falling from the tree and the consequent dreadful punishment that followed was well worth it because I wouldn't ever have to wear it again.

The snowdrop, however, was another matter. I'd had my eye on this particular snowdrop for some time. I'd noticed it when it had first begun to appear because for some reason it was on its own.

It was a lone snowdrop that grew quite proudly on the banking of grass beside the garden gate. It had just appeared and that was that. But its arrival brought much joy and excitement to our household. It was the first of its kind and there was a general hope and expectation that if it wasn't interfered with, it would increase in number in years to come. Not only did the family gather around it in homage, but every visitor, either on arrival or departure, was encouraged to praise its solitary presence and particular beauty.

I just wish someone had praised *my* solitary presence and beauty sometimes. My legs were just as white and delicate as that rotten snowdrop, a least they were until the smacks began again. Then they took on that rosy glow that indicated they had received another belting.

I'd been told not to pick it but I did. No one could prove anything because I'd thrown it into a hedge so it couldn't be seen. I don't know why I got the blame. No one had actually seen me do it. I was going to give it to my mum as a present, but had thought better of it. So, having picked it, I chucked it and that was the end of it. Except I came in for another belting and all because of that rotten snowdrop. After that I stuck to dandelions, there were more of them and my mum seemed to like them better. She said I could pick as many of them as I liked and so for several days I had white legs.

Chapel

The chapel was attended as a duty every Sunday morning. I recall at an early age trying to climb the stone steps on my own up to the chapel vestibule and trying to see over the pew in front to find out if it was a visiting preacher.

They were called lay-preachers and in later life, I confessed to my father, who was the resident minister, that I thought they were called 'lay' because of their ability to lay most of the congregation to sleep in a very short space of time.

In those days thirty-five minutes was a short sermon, but those who preached on David and Goliath, as many did, I certainly had time for. This to me was a sermon about someone my size getting his own back, in a very simple way, against someone twice as big who wanted to clobber him.

The story is open to misinterpretation and many, many years later I heard an American evangelist ask five-year-old Emily Johnson, what, if anything, the story has to tell us. Quick as a flash she replied "Duck!"

Long sermons were expected and they were often heavy and pedantic in those days. I often wondered if the visiting preachers were trying to justify their five-shilling fee. Perhaps if they'd been paid less their sermons might have been briefer!

Chapel was part of my life and the life of the family. We were taken there every Sunday morning and I suppose because of those early encounters, I've never known a life without God. But there are times when I question his motives and his justice.

I was sitting next to my mother and I recall she wasn't in a particularly good mood that morning. I was fed up with sitting on the pew and so was very restless. As a mere innocent, I tried to pass the time in some sort of valuable way. I'd looked at the ladies' hats, thumbed through the pages of a hymn book, kicked my feet on the pew in front and had accidently broken wind, though only very slightly. On feeling the wrath and impatience of my mother brewing and seeing her rise to her feet I lurched into the aisle and ran as fast as I could to the front of the chapel. I leapt over the communion rail, climbed up the steps of the pulpit and joined my father who was just beginning his sermon.

He was a bit surprised but being a patient individual let me stand next to him as he addressed the congregation. It wasn't long before I began to mimic his every word and gesture through the spaces between the bars of the pulpit front. This was too much for my mother who by now had tiptoed her way in my direction, grabbed me firmly from behind and taken me by the scruff of my neck out of the chapel and home.

Once there I was sat upon the kitchen table, where my shoes were removed, my legs smacked and I was sent to bed. The signs of my sins and their punishments were to be seen once again in my pink legs and I've been rather nervous of pulpits ever since.

God's Lack of Interest in Bottoms

I've always found it rather sad that some Christians have no sense of humour and many years later my nervousness of them was confirmed. I was in Sunday school where I was sent every Sunday, probably to give my parents some respite. We learnt of God through rhymes and jingles and Bible stories but I must admit I didn't particularly enjoy it because it was rather dull.

It was run by a very austere lady called Miss Hood. How that name suited her. She was tall and very thin and looked as though she ought to wear a hood like one of those mysterious characters who used to roam the grounds of Greyfriars at night in my sister's comic, 'School Friend'.

We were sitting on long wooden benches in rows listening to her going on about those who "saw the splinter in another's eye when they had a beam in theirs" and we, who had already become restless, were pushing ourselves to the right along the bench to see if we could force the one at the end to fall off. Now, the thing about these benches was that you sat still or like me you reaped the consequences.

"Miss, oh Miss," I said as I put my hand up into the air, "I've got a splinter in my bottom."

A huge success with lots of laughter and giggles from the girls. But not Miss Hood.

"Andrew Woodhouse," she said. "God is not interested in bottoms!"

So I learnt a profound lesson and my first theological truth, that there is one area, at least, in this universe that God avoids.

Chapel Sunday School

Father Christmas Stops Off

Christmas was always a time of great joy and expectation. The lead up to Christmas was full of mystery and magic and spicy aromas that came from my mother's baking and cooking in preparation for the festive season.

We all loved Christmas and it truly was a season of goodwill, but my first introduction to Father Christmas wasn't a good one and for many years afterwards I used to approach anyone claiming to be Father Christmas, St Nicholas, Santa Claus or just plain old Santa with great caution. I was told in later life that it was all to do with the war, with shortages and all that, but then the war was blamed for a lot and Christmas need not have been so traumatic even during the war. At least not in rural Suffolk.

The trouble was that I had been schooled for weeks about this red-coated, generous present-giving Father Christmas just like the one in my story book. But this one was the real one and he was coming to the chapel school room at four o'clock just as the tea party was about to end and if I was a good boy then he'd give me a special present.

We were back at the chapel again for the Christmas party. At four years old I took all this in, although I did wonder in my childish understanding of events that of all the exotic destinations in the world he considered our chapel schoolroom one of the most important on his world tour.

Nevertheless, as promised there he was at four o'clock precisely and although I was a bit apprehensive, I was thrust upon his knee and he asked me what I'd like for Christmas. I mumbled something about keeping my legs white which he didn't seem to understand. But what was really beginning to trouble me was that he appeared to have a hole in his beard. Well actually it was his cheek, he had a hole in his cheek!

Years later I realised that he must have been wearing a paper facial mask of some kind. Anyway, I found the hole, lined it up in my sights and poked it with my outstretched finger, much to the dismay of the elderly ladies of the chapel choir, dressed in Lincoln green, who were pretending to be Santa's little elves as they sang carols ever so softly. The whole event only lasted a couple of minutes but it left a lasting impression on me and I avoided any further contact with Father Christmas for a very long time.

The present I received? A few coloured cardboard shapes that could be formed into different patterns. Hardly worth his trip really.

My sister fared much better as he'd given her a cotton purse. Unfortunately, there was no money in it. I tried to do a swop with her but she wouldn't. So we went to bed and dreamt of better things for Christmas Day.

A Little Accident

It started as a little trickle and my sister saw it first. I couldn't hold it back any longer and I could see from the pain in my sister's eyes she felt so sorry for me and knew I'd get into trouble. I loved my sister very much and at times like this I wished she'd been sitting next to me so I could hold her hand and try to stem the flow.

My sister Margaret had always been a real pal to me. She had nice white legs like mine but she used to keep hers white because she was always good, at least we all thought so. She had lovely long black curled hair, almost down the length of her back and brown eyes any film star would be proud of. She knew as well as I did that anyone who wet their pants in class was in for real trouble. We were instructed to go at playtime because Miss Rope, the head of this private "caring" infant school had declared it but I hadn't been.

Miss Rope wasn't very tall but to us she was formidable and not to be reckoned with. She was a scrawny looking woman and she had a pointed nose that could sniff out trouble at a hundred yards. Unfortunately, I was well within that distance and it wasn't long before her gaze moved away from the story book from which she was reading to survey her pupils.

We were sitting in a circle and her attention had been drawn to the fact that the children on either side of me had begun to shuffle their chairs away from where I was sitting. She rose from her chair, put her book down and stood in front of me her hands on her hips.

"And what do you think you are doing?" she asked.

"Nothing Miss, I'm not doing anything, honest!"

By now she had come up behind me and I thought, "O Lord, here it comes." She grabbed the back of my shirt collar and hoisted me up out of my damp patch, as though I was a fish on the end of a line and she propelled me towards the door of the classroom and out onto the path that led to the outside toilets.

All the way along the path she thumped me in the middle of my back and when we arrived at the toilet door she told me to open it. She seemed very angry. But I couldn't open the door because the handle was too far up, so after several attempts at jumping to reach it, I gave up.

"You dirty little boy," she said. "You dirty little boy."

The offending wet pants were removed and I was given a very old and threadbare pair of trousers to put on which were too long and I was returned to the classroom by the same route with the same thumps in the middle of my back.

My return was greeted in silence and all the children were still sitting in the circle looking very superior at the one who had returned from wetting his pants. They all looked down their noses at me apart from my sister Margaret and I detected a tear in her eye.

As my sister and I walked home from school that night we were accompanied by an older girl called Kathleen who used to come to my dad for violin lessons. The three of us must have looked quite comical. Kathleen swinging her violin case and Margaret swinging a large paper carrier bag in which were deposited the still damp pants which she'd been given because I couldn't be trusted with them. I had to follow behind in my recently acquired antiquated trousers. Kathleen was being really mean, talking about what had happened to me all the way home.

"You'll be in right trouble tonight when you get home, when your Mum finds out what you've done. Fancy wetting your pants!"

And so she went on and I felt more and more ashamed of myself and in fear of what was yet to come until my dear sister told her to shut up and leave me alone. How lovely to have such a champion for my cause by my side.

When we arrived home my sister dashed into the kitchen with the large paper bag and I heard her mumbling in deep conversation with my mother. I don't know what she said but instead of a beating my mother came out of the kitchen and gave me a big hug and a jam tart. She also tried very hard to hold back from laughing uncontrollably when she caught sight of my latest fashion in trousers.

Johnnie Smelt

In the yearly cycle of events the Chapel Anniversary was a significant and very special social occasion in the life of the chapel. I was now nearly six years of age and I was encouraged, almost bullied, by my mother to make a real contribution to it. My dad she assured me would be very proud of me.

I wasn't really quite sure what it was all about but something special was afoot and being planned on a big scale. Large women always seemed to be in our house, talking non-stop around my mother who was constantly walking around with a piece of paper in her hand. Whereas my father gave the impression of being fairly distant and appeared to walk in a different direction from her but in passing nodded with an approving glance. What a strange world I seemed to be living in but I just had a feeling I was going to be involved with all of this and I wasn't wrong.

Sometime later my mother knelt down beside me and said she thought this year I was old enough to make a little contribution to the service in the chapel with all the other boys and girls who would be taking part. She said she had a nice little poem that I could recite. I didn't think this was a good idea because I couldn't memorise anything and even to this day I can't remember scripts. However, here she was with this poem which she would help me recite from memory. I recall the words even today:

> Johnnie smelt a pretty rose
> That grew in Mummy's garden
> The sharp thorns pricked his little nose
> And never begged his pardon

Well hardly words to captivate an audience at The Old Vic, but good enough to present for the Chapel Anniversary and no doubt my mother expected me to earn one or two oohs and aahs and "bless hims" after my first solo performance. So I learnt it, with great difficulty I might add. But I did, even though I had problems with remembering the third line.

All primed and ready to go, the great day arrived and dusted down and made to look presentable, off to chapel we went. There was quite a large choir sitting on a small stage at the front of the chapel and various people were shuffling into their places. I was placed on a small chair at the side of the choir and left on my own but I think my mother thought better of it as she took my hand and sat me next to her in the main body of the congregation. Eventually my father came in and ascended the pulpit steps. He gave a little talk that seemed to praise everyone including the Almighty and we were then into the first hymn. Everything was going well and I was quite enjoying the proceedings, lulled into thinking that chapel wasn't too bad after all, when suddenly it was announced that I was to recite my special poem. Those in the pews immediately to the front and to the right of us turned and gave a strange mixture of encouraging smiles and looked at my mother to see the pride in her face. Pride in hers maybe, but not in mine.

"Go on," she said, "go on it's you. Off you go." She looked around and smiled at everyone.

"Go on," she said, "go to the front and say what you've learnt."

Reluctantly I slid forward from my pew and very gingerly wandered down the aisle which seemed to be a mile long into the silence of the waiting audience. Silence is what I remember most and a sea of faces, some friendly and some not so friendly.

Oh dear I couldn't remember my words, they'd gone. I faced the congregation and saw my mother now sitting on the edge of her pew willing me to perform well. I thought if I don't get it right this time I'm really for it and my legs will be pink for a week.

"Johnnie smelt…"

I can't remember it!

"Johnnie smelt…"

Why are people beginning to giggle?

"Johnnie smelt..."

Why is everyone now looking towards Johnnie Peterson and why is he looking at me so menacingly? I'll try again.

"Johnnie smelt a......pretty rose......that......grew in Mummy's garden. The sharp thorns pricked his little nose and never begged his pardon."

I bowed and received rapturous applause for having managed to finish it. I ran back to the shelter of my mum who wrapped her arms around me and I knew she was quite pleased with my first venture into public speaking.

Later my dad said, "Well done son you did your best."

That was praise indeed.

He went on to say "With a voice like that I can see you in the pulpit one day just like your Dad."

Such prophecy! As I lay in bed that night I thought about how I had captured the real meaning of that poem in the first two words.

Mother

A New Wheelbarrow

My sixth birthday arrived and I was given a beautiful gleaming green wooden wheelbarrow. It had been specially made for me by a friend of my father. I really *wanted* a wheelbarrow, I've no idea why. Perhaps it was because my father had an allotment some distance from the house and I used to enjoy going there with him.

He used to carry his gardening tools on his shoulders and I'd walk beside him and we'd chat along the way. I remember the path we walked along was strewn with all kinds of wild flowers. When the vegetables on the allotment were ready to eat we used to gather them and carry them home in bags and buckets and my father had suggested that I should have a wheel barrow and then I could help carry some too.

I thought it was a great idea and so I asked if I could have one for my birthday and here it was all green and shiny and bright. It was quite a thrill to take it down to the allotment as I felt like a real gardener. As it tumbled over the rough paths, its wooden wheel bouncing on the cobblestones and pebbles, what joy I had. When we loaded it up with vegetables to take home to my mother I was very pleased.

It seems strange that I knew nothing at that time of the brave men and women who were sacrificing their lives across the channel so that I was able to have such a happy childhood. I'll always salute their memory and bravery. It was a very joyful period of my life, being able to share these precious moments with my father who was often otherwise far too busy with his work as a Minister of the Church.

Coming home from the allotment one day we noticed a great deal of smoke rising into the sky ahead of us. It was more than smoke caused by a bonfire. We hurried to see what it was all about. My father was very concerned and I was a bit apprehensive myself. It had been a very hot day and the long grass in the garden of a house had caught fire and had spread to the woodshed which was now in flames.

Everything seemed to be in confusion. Water was spurting up from the punctured hose pipes of the fire engines and firemen were shouting out directions at the top of their voices, some from the very tops of the fire engines while some took up brooms and spades and were attempting to put out the burning grass.

I remember standing at the side of the garden with my sister watching the flames getting closer to our feet every second. My father put both of us inside a greenhouse where I presume he thought that we would be quite safe. Shortly afterwards they brought in a white-haired old gentleman and sat him down on a rickety old chair next to us. They left him there and my sister and I gazed at him wondering who he was. We were chatting to him about the fire for some time and he seemed a very kind old gentleman but he looked very worried.

Suddenly he gave a sort of sigh and he didn't speak to us anymore. My sister and I looked at each other and wondered why he had suddenly gone very quiet. We didn't know at the time but he must have had a heart attack and died. After a while a very tall and slender lady came into the greenhouse to see how we all were. Taking a quick look at the three of us she ushered my sister and myself out of the greenhouse and onto the lane and my father took us by the hand and led us home. As we approached the bend in the lane a big white van with a red cross on the side and a ringing bell shot past us very quickly. Later that night we guessed that the old man had been taken ill. My sister said he had died but I didn't want to believe her. But that night I saw him in my dreams and he was smiling at us from the gates of heaven. In the morning I told my mother about the dream.

"That's nice dear," she said.

When we went to the allotment again I looked into the garden and it was very black and nothing could be seen to be growing. I looked for the old man but I didn't see him.

"He must have gone to heaven after all," I said.

The Magical Gramophone

When the sun shone in those lazy days of summer we used to go for picnics to Thorpeness, a sheltered seaside cove within easy walking distance. It was a very pretty place with sand dunes and long grasses where we could sit and play in the sand.

Swimming was not allowed because all along the edge of the sea were rolls upon rolls of barbed wire, put there to thwart any attempts by the enemy to land on our coastline. To us this was all quite normal because we had never really seen any seashore without the inevitable barbed wire. I don't think it would have had much effect on stemming German stormtroopers though but I suppose it was good for moral and gave the coastguard something to warn us about if we strayed too near it in our attempt to dip a toe into the sea.

I remember too the blasting of aircraft guns, especially in the night, that gave us all the reassurance that they were defending our homes as we tried to sleep.

Nights were always interrupted, either by the air raid siren waking us all or by my father moving us from our comfortable beds to under the stairs for more protection. This was a precaution but it made my sister and I very afraid.

Sometimes we would hear the bombers overhead on their way to the docks or some other unfortunate place and we cowered under our blankets thanking God they were not after us this particular night and saying a silent prayer for the poor victims and their families. Even at this early age I felt a great sympathy for those who were suffering as a result of this horrid war and wished it was all over.

My sister and I often wondered what it would be like to live in a peaceful world, for up until then we had known nothing but a time of war. One night an incendiary bomb landed in our garden and Dad and a neighbour rushed out with a bucket and hose pipe to dowse it.

My dad got his training in civil defence at the R.A.F. station up the road where he was a chaplain. As he was a Minister of Religion he didn't fight on the front. I asked him if he had a gun which was a silly question really as I couldn't imagine Dad shooting anyone. He said he'd never had a gun but that he had a whistle. Now I found this very amusing, to think there was only a whistle between him and the advancing Germans. Apparently it was used a bit like a policeman's whistle as a warning or to summon help. I wasn't impressed.

When I was a child it was the usual routine to bathe twice a week and in some ways it was a bit of a performance. On this winter's night because it was too cold upstairs in the bathroom the ablutions were to take place in the kitchen. Soap, towels, pyjamas and dressing gown were set out ready. I wasn't willing at all to have a bath in a cold kitchen sitting in a square pot sink. I found the whole procedure undignified and it was very cold.

"Get in this sink now!" my mother's voice of authority and……here we go again……pink legs! Screams and tears and more screams and tears I could really shake the foundations when I tried. But I was hoisted into the sink still screaming out and just managed to cover my eyes with a face cloth before the dreaded hair washing took place. When I emerged from my ordeal I was amazed to see two soldiers in full battle dress standing at the ready advancing in my direction. They said they'd heard all the noise and commotion and thought the second front had begun. I started to laugh again and so did they.

Apparently they had called to see Dad and he had told them to come in and surprise me.

The following day something remarkable happened. After my bath episode the house had returned to its normal functioning, but during the day I had a feeling that something was in the air. Dad had been on one of his church visitations and had been out most of the day. Round about tea time my mother kept looking out of the front window to see if Dad was coming up the drive, she hardly ever did this, so I wondered why she was so anxious today to see him home. My sister and I were suddenly ushered into the kitchen and told to wait there until mother came for us as we were in for a surprise.

We heard Dad arrive and it sounded like he had someone with him. There was a murmur of voices in the hallway and then we were allowed out to see what was going on. There in the hall alongside Dad was our brother David who had come home for the holidays from boarding school. He used to be away from home for so long that we almost forgot about him sometimes. But there he was and we were glad to be all together again.

When we went into the dining room however, my sister and I noticed a large blue box in the middle of the floor. It certainly hadn't been there during the day and we presumed that it had arrived with Dad and David. So it had, but what was it?

On closer inspection it appeared to be hinged and had a small hole in its side. It wasn't very interesting at all so we decided to wander off and find something else to do before tea.

But this box unknown to us held more magic than I could ever imagine. When Dad lifted it onto a little table and opened it up we could see a round turntable and a sort of silver coloured arm with a pointed needle in it.

"This," he said, "is a gramophone. I've had it in my study for a long time. It had a broken spring but I've had it repaired and now it plays. Listen to this." He then took out a handle placed it into the side of the box and wound it up. Placing a record on the turntable he gently lowered the arm and we had music.

It was magic, simply magic. I hadn't heard anything like it before. There in our dining room playing with all they could muster was the band of the Scots Guards. When the record had finished we pleaded for it to be played again, but we were told we had to have our tea first. But, if we were very, very, good and got ready for bed and put on our pyjamas without making a fuss we could stay up and listen to more of the records Dad had in his little collection.

That night I was as good as gold and we had a wonderful and memorable evening sitting around the embers of the fire. It was a night I'll never forget. Our family was complete, and we were content to let the music drift on into the night.

A Downed Aircraft

We were very fortunate to live in the country, but we didn't escape the war. One morning as I was walking to school with my dad and sister we heard a terrible noise overhead. It was like the sound of shrieking and clanging. We all looked up and saw an aircraft with flames and smoke issuing out of its tail and my dad said, "That's been hit." We tried to follow its path up in the sky but we lost it. It was a bit scary and we listened for an explosion as it hit the ground but we didn't hear anything. Later we learned from my mum that the plane and crew had managed to land safely.

We reached school and my sister and I were treated a bit like celebrities, for we had seen what the others had only been told about this aircraft in distress. We were in demand to give a graphic account and I think we exaggerated it all maybe a tiny bit.

We seemed to have our fair share of air raid warnings throughout the school day which were sometimes a blessing to me. I very much disliked PE lessons. I saw no use or benefit in them whatsoever. I just couldn't see the point in taking off the top half of your clothes, in my case a vest, as well as my shirt. I always had to wear a vest, to keep out the cold. I suppose that wasn't too bad although some of the other boys giggled a bit to each other when they saw me taking off my fancy attire.

I was a bit concerned when I noticed my sister was wearing a vest similar to mine with rubber buttons up the front. She called hers a liberty bodice. Surely my mother wouldn't send me to school wearing one of those. Only later did I discover that it certainly was one of my sister's liberty bodices and I was mortified. My mother apparently thought it would be a snug fit and the buttons when fastened would keep me warmer.

She had some strange ideas when it came to keeping me warm. Thermogene was another one of them. This was an orange prickly material a bit like cotton wool but it irritated the skin greatly. It was supposed to generate heat like a cold poultice and so it did, but at great cost. She used to put it in a large wad between the shoulders of my liberty bodice and skin. The irritation was unbearable as it heated the area around and spread to other tender parts. It was hard to think about anything especially school work when you were so irritated. Removing the top half of my clothes for PE at least gave me the opportunity to get rid of the Thermogene as I casually kicked it under a table.

I was ready at last in just my short trousers and braces waiting for our lesson to begin. I found the whole exercise so utterly boring and a complete waste of time. I could never work out the untold benefits of flinging your arms high above your head and jumping up in the air at the same time or standing with legs apart and touching the floor without bending your knees.

I was reprimanded every time because I wasn't able to do it without bending mine.

"Come along Andrew, you really must try harder!"

I was sure most of the other children had shorter legs to enable them to do it so easily.

Then there was the so-called fun game of standing opposite a partner and throwing a bean bag to each other which we were supposed to catch. I couldn't manage that either and consequently I was often the last person picked for any team game that took place outside on the field. I learnt to accept this because I wasn't interested in any kind of team game.

When PE lessons came around I longed for the air raid siren to sound and when it did, and it did fairly often, I silently thanked the Luftwaffe and grabbing my liberty bodice and shirt made for the shelter where I knew I could sit awhile, snooze or look at a picture book. All of these activities were much more enjoyable than trying to do the impossible with my arms and legs.

Art was a most enjoyable lesson. We were often expected to produce a masterpiece using a few bits of old chalk on a well-worn piece of slate. These slates squeaked when you drew on them and they were so tiny you finished a drawing very swiftly. I didn't like using them at all and tried to produce something as fast as I could. I drew anything as long as it looked like something.

"That looks like a nice drawing Andrew, what is it?"

I'd look at it and make up a name as close to the image as I could. Often I said it was our house because that seemed to be an acceptable title for everything.

"Well done, Andrew. Would you like to give out the milk and biscuits at playtime?"

Of course I would because that meant I could have first choice of the biscuits!

When we painted we were given a sheet of clean paper, a clean water pot and brush. The brushes were sometimes a bit worn but were a pleasant change to the bits of broken chalk. The paint was made of powder and the colours were put into bun trays. You had to put your brush into the water and then into the paint to transfer the colour to your paper. Round plates were used to mix the colours and altogether this was an enjoyable experience.

We were told not to waste the paint as it was in short supply and so we painted very carefully. I always started off enthusiastically and really enjoyed myself but after a while my painting seemed to become a bit of a mess. My sister would say that I was a bit silly sometimes. And I was. She however, was quite brilliant at making lovely countryside scenes and painting faces of people. They were so well painted her work was always praised. At least all *her* pictures were instantly recognisable.

King Arthur

I spent my childhood in an era before computers, CDs, teletext, internet and mobile phones. There were no televisions and few radios. We had to make our own entertainment and when we weren't busy being mischievous we could be quite creative. It was a time when we entered our own world of fantasy, fairy tales and legends and where the counterpane of the bed became the rolling hills of Camelot. Here I galloped my Bakelite horses making the appropriate noises as St George and I embarked upon our journey to fight the dragon I had hidden at the bottom of the bed.

Other times it was King Arthur and his knights who were rescuing fair maidens in distress. The fair maiden being any old doll that happened to be lying about the bedroom looking as though she was at a loose end. What jolly days they were.

For some days my mother had been busy with cardboard boxes and odd bits of cardboard and string trying to make some kind of knight's outfit. She had already made a very impressive breastplate and shield and now she was busy making a magnificent helmet with see-through visor and adjustable lid.

The chapel were holding a fancy dress competition and knowing my fondness for Arthur my mother had decided I should go, if not as Arthur, then at least as one of his knights. My father produced a wonderful wooden sword and I pondered on its capability as a really good weapon. I was really looking forward to wearing my costume and taking part in the event.

My sister who I thought was quite pretty made a very satisfactory Guinevere, although it did cross my mind later as we entered the procession together that Pauline Clarke, who was dressed as a sunflower, may slightly have had the edge on her.

The event was held outdoors in a field and that was its undoing. As the heavens suddenly opened my cardboard breast plate, helmet and see-through visor with adjustable lid were no match for the cloudburst and throwing my sword on the ground in disgust I squelched off the field like a thoroughly *papier-mâché* Arthur, unrecognisable and ruined.

In later years whenever I've read or talked on the text of St Paul's "Put on the whole armour of God" from his letter to the Ephesians I recall that cloudburst and I smile. We made the effort Paul. It's just that the weather was against us.

Chapel Outing

Motor transport was not readily available during the war years so our chapel Sunday School outing needed to be arranged as a day out with a difference. My mother seemed to spend the whole of the previous evening preparing a picnic for this great excursion and was still on with it as my sister and I were ushered off to bed. Sleep was hard to come by as we were both so excited about the thought of the next day's adventures. We'd no idea where we were heading for or where the picnic was to take place but it was such a pleasant interruption in our day to day lives we were so happy.

Morning came and the sun was shining. Everyone seemed to be in a cheery mood and I just had a little thought that today I might keep out of trouble. After we had early breakfast, we all waited by the garden gate for our transport to arrive. Soon a distant rumble of voices and clanking of wheels could be heard coming nearer and nearer and louder and louder. Eventually over the brow of the hill a pair of horses heads could be seen and behind them emerged very slowly a rickety old farm cart full of children and rather stout ladies and elderly men dressed in their Sunday best. When the cart pulled up and we were invited to take our places I could see that the seats were made up of the long wooden benches out of the chapel schoolroom. These had been placed back to back and tied together with binder twine and were positioned down the middle of the cart.

Everyone seemed to have a jolly time talking to each other and some began to sing songs and my father pointed out various wild flowers to me and my sister as we all trundled along the lanes to our unknown destination.

At some point in the proceedings I had a small bag of sweets thrust into my hands which was a surprise and I ate them one after another in case I was expected to hand them around.

When the cart eventually ground to a halt the cry went up "Everybody out!" and one by one we were helped down by the kindly driver.

Holding my mother's hand, off we went to find the sea. I found myself jumping and sliding into the sand dunes and then there it was. The sea. The sea!

"This is lovely," she giggled, "what a view. I can't wait to dip my feet in the water and feel the sand between my toes."

My father had put a knotted handkerchief onto his head and had begun to pull silly faces.

"Don't do that," said my mum, "people will think you're daft."

I was already beginning to think that myself.

Then Isabel was sick. Her mum said it was probably the excitement and the bumpy cart, another boy Peter looked very pale and Pauline looked radiant but tired, so it was decided to settle on the sand dunes and have lunch first before organising any games.

Games? It was a word that filled me with dread. I hated any kind of running, jumping, leaping up and down or even standing on the spot if it was classed as games. I was no good at physical activities because I didn't enjoy it and whenever there was a team to pick and I was an option, my name was always called last accompanied by a groan from the other team members.

The picnic lunch was really good. It was supposed to be made up of wartime rations but we still had a sausage and a piece of pork pie, and lots of egg sandwiches. We also had a very splendid cake with icing on top as a final treat. All this and a glass or two of ginger pop left me pleasantly full and a little sleepy and as the sun was up and quite hot by now I fell into a warm and contented snooze. I woke to the sound of my name being called and opening my eyes saw a pair of freckled legs.

"Are you coming? We're playing cricket."

I glanced up and recognised Pauline. Only she could smile that way and speak with such a gentle persuasive tone.

"Cricket? I don't know how to play that!" I said.

"Don't worry we'll soon show you."

So rubbing the sleep from my eyes I followed her down to the shore and I was put in a team and told to field. I had never fielded before and had no idea what I was supposed to be doing.

"I don't know what to do."

"Watch me!" cried a rather tall girl, "try to catch the ball."

So I stood there trying to look interested and enthusiastic but all the time wished that I had remained in the safe haven next to my mother. Only once did the ball come by me and I missed it although it was travelling at a snail's pace.

"Oh, well tried! Next time put your foot out and stop it that way."

Eventually the team that was batting was out and now it was our turn. I seemed to stand around for ages whilst the others hit the ball all over the place. But at last my name was called and I was given a bat.

"Try your best and I'll send you a gentle ball," called the old gentleman who was standing a way in front of me "here it comes!"

And there it went as far as I was concerned. I missed it. "Never mind, try again."

My dad stepped up behind me and held my bat steady, clasping his hands around mine.

"Ready?" asked Dad and up went the bat and caught the ball square on and it flew high into the air and well across the sands.

"Wow!" I cried.

"Six!" everyone shouted and I ran as fast as I could like the others.

"Stop!" they all cried, "you don't have to run for a six." So I stopped and so did the game as my six gave us a win. "Good old Dad," I thought, "he can hit them when he wants to."

After all that excitement we wandered along the beach gathering shells and bits of seaweed until the horses were fed and watered and we set off again for home.

The homeward journey would have been uneventful apart from the storm that broke. Suddenly the weather changed and the rain came down and though everyone tried to put things above their heads to keep off the rain, nothing did and we arrived home wet through so we said our goodbyes very swiftly and squelched our way up the garden path. What a happy day it had been and how I was praised for hitting that six.

After my sister and I were tucked up in our beds that night I relived the day in my dreams. I thought of that old rickety cart full of happy faces, that lovely picnic and the little snooze I'd had in those friendly sand dunes and Pauline's beguiling smile. I'd played my first game of cricket and scored the winning six.

The Victory Parade

The war eventually came to an end and this was a time of great celebration. I had never known such happiness in our household. Everyone was fantastically good humoured and seemed to want to celebrate in any way they could. My father danced around with a tea cosy on his head and my mother opened a tin of peaches that she said she was saving for a special occasion and what better occasion could there be than this.

My gran seemed to be in the kitchen all day baking cakes for tea. "There will be a lot more of these," she said, "now the war's over." We all cheered. We did a lot of cheering that day.

There was to be a great pageant in the town with marching bands, floats and fancy dress. It seemed everyone was going to take part and that, of course, meant myself and my sister Margaret. I wondered what we would be dressed in this time. The clever nimble fingers of my mother produced a nurses outfit for my sister and I must say she looked very authentic. I myself was the wounded soldier.

I was given a crutch to put under my arm and there was a bandage on one of my legs, so I limped along in the procession with great enthusiasm, although I think now and again I limped on the wrong foot when my concentration lapsed.

That was the last I remember of that idyllic life in the countryside because shortly afterwards I was told that we were all going to uproot and move to Sheffield. This news came as a bit of a shock to me. Apparently, my father thought a new church in new surroundings was a good idea and he'd been off to apply for the vacancy at The Wicker Congregational Church. Having made a reasonable impression to all and sundry he'd decided to accept the invitation to go there, so off we were going. This wasn't good news to me and I knew I'd miss the lovely countryside and even the snowdrops at the bottom of the garden that had increased in number.

Nurse and wounded soldier 1945

Hello Sheffield

I was interested in how everything was to be packed, especially the furniture. However, my sister Margaret and I were to travel to Brimington near Chesterfield with Gran to stay for a few days with an Aunt Clara, so I never did find out.

The day arrived and we said our goodbyes to that lovely house and set off by train to Chesterfield. It seemed a long journey and I fell asleep. I was awakened rather abruptly by my gran.

"Come on our Andrew wake up. We're here."

Grabbing what bits of luggage I thought I could carry I more or less fell off the train and was greeted rather over enthusiastically by an old man who I found out later was an Uncle Fred, married to my gran's sister. He had an enormous nose that pointed to one side and I couldn't stop myself looking at it and thinking, "I bet he can tell if anyone's cooking cabbage in Sheffield!"

Aunt Clara reminded me of Mother Riley. Whatever she was doing she seemed to wriggle all over the place. Her house seemed quite poor compared to the old country house we had left. I remember the staircase being very steep and the bed was covered in a feather mattress. I had to share this with my sister.

"You'll manage for a couple of nights." Gran said.

But we didn't. The bed springs had given up the ghost many years before and consequently when you got into bed the mattress came up and clouted you on the side of your head. I knew I'd either die of concussion or by suffocation in the night. My sister just told me to shut up and stop making a fuss.

There wasn't much to do during the daytime. However, we were told not to converse with the lady next door. In fact, we were told to keep out of her way because she swore a lot.

Well that seemed a good enough reason for me to keep a watchful eye out for her as I was really curious to hear what she had to say. It could after all brighten up what could be a dull day. I didn't have to wait long. I saw her back door open ever so slightly one morning and then suddenly a big black dog ran out. It flew like a mad thing all the way up the street as though it was being chased by the devil. Now, I don't know what the real name of that dog was, but I'm sure it wasn't all the names it was called that morning.

Gran flew out of our back door and pulled me inside.

"You didn't hear all that, did you?"

"No, Gran I didn't."

What a silly question. What sort of reply did she expect? Of course I did and it was worth waiting for!

We were apparently in walking distance of two more sets of Aunts and Uncles so it was not surprising that we all trooped off to visit them.

The first house we called at contained an Aunt Edith and an Uncle Arthur. Arthur was Gran's brother, he was a tall lanky looking man and after the first hello's I noticed he sat down on his chair with his long legs wrapped around each other in a most peculiar way, a bit like a deformed Daddy Longlegs.

His saving grace was that he painted the most beautiful landscape pictures I'd ever seen. On later visits to their house he let me paint alongside him and perhaps that had an influence on my love of painting in later life.

Edith was a very meek and mild individual who hardly spoke unless she was spoken to and even then seemed to be afraid that she had said the wrong thing. Arthur gave me the impression that he could be a bit of a bully and I kept my distance.

They had a daughter, my cousin Kathleen, who was so pleased to see us all and was quite excitable. She gave me the impression that she thought I was a bit of a lad and I took advantage of that by saying kind things to her that made her blush uncontrollably.

She was a very pretty girl and she surprised us all by singing to us as we had tea and cakes. She had the most beautiful voice in the world and could soar effortlessly to the highest realms any voice could reach. Her voice was heavenly. She'd been given a great gift. Some years later when she lost her life so tragically in a road traffic accident something inside of me died as well. But I still hear her voice and listen to her songs as she sings in heaven.

We had to call in to see the other Aunts and Uncles as we were in the vicinity and so it was we arrived at our next destination to be greeted by Uncle Fred, the one with the long bent nose and an Aunt Alice, another of Gran's sisters. We had tea at their house and we were joined by another Uncle Fred and Aunt Lily. I'm not sure if they were a real Aunt and Uncle but that was how they were introduced.

The tea was a bit disappointing. By now I was starving and bread and jam followed by tinned fruit was hardly menu of the year.

During the process of having tea I couldn't help noticing that Aunt Lily had a bit of a strange incapacity. Whenever someone asked her to pass something across the table she couldn't do so without her hand shaking. She had very thin hands almost in the shape of a claw that emphasised her action.

Everyone else pretended not to notice, but I did and I latched onto this as a means of lightening up the boredom of this very proper tea party. In fact, I asked her continually to pass things to the point that my sister and I got the giggles. I also passed a few things to my sister and held my hand in the shape of a claw. She was bursting to laugh. I was able to keep a perfectly straight face and a look of innocence as I completed all this mischief. An ability I retained throughout my life. No one realised why we were giggling and thought we were just enjoying ourselves. That is everyone except Gran who later said I was a bad lad.

My father knew of dear Aunt Lily's disability and there were occasions when we had people for tea and when they weren't looking I'd pass him something with the claw hand and the shake. It always had the desired effect of making him laugh and he too said I was a bad lad.

Anyway after tea we had to endure a conducted tour of Uncle Fred's allotment and the problems he had with wayward rabbits and then it was time to return to Aunt Sarah.

It had been a long day. I don't think I'd ever met so many relatives in such a short time. As we approached Aunt Sara's the lady next door was in the street.

"Bloody dog's out again."

Andrew & Margaret, Sheffield

A New House

The next day we were on our way to the new house at Sheffield. Having said goodbye to all our new found relatives who had waved us off at the railway station we eagerly looked forward to the prospect of fresh surroundings and our first glimpse of Sheffield.

It was an industrial base for iron and steel works and before we could see it we could smell it.

"Poo, what a pong." I said, "What's that?"

"It must be the smell of the iron works" said Gran.

Good grief, I thought, if Sheffield smells like that you can keep it! The pong was still in the air as we were met at the station by yet another uncle I'd never met before.

"This is your Uncle Charlie," said Gran. He's my son.

"How are you Charlie?"

"Alright Ma. They're waiting for you all up at the house. I think you'll like it. We'll take a taxi."

On the way I got my first glimpse of an industrial city that seemed very foreboding and alien to anything I'd seen before. The whole city seemed to be encased in a grey fog and there were lots of derelict bombed buildings and some looked as though they'd been on fire.

Onwards we sped and eventually we stopped halfway up a hill outside of a house that had laurel bushes overhanging the wall. There were countless steps up to the front door where Mum and Dad stood to greet us.

"You made it then?"

Immediately there followed the usual tour of the house. Mum said that they'd spent most of their time over the last few days taking tacks out of the floorboards. We all agreed that it would need to be completely re-decorated. The whole house had been painted in bottle green and dark brown glossy paint. What a mess. I didn't like this house one little bit and wanted to go back to our home in the country.

We had to settle into it but looking back I don't think any of us really became attached to that house. It had three stories with a large dusty attic. There was a passageway that ran along one side of the house and a small back yard and a great long patch of garden beyond that seemed to attract all the cats in the area. The kitchen was very old-fashioned with an old range. It took Gran, even with all her expertise, several attempts to get it going. Beyond the kitchen was a scullery where the weekly washing was to take place without fail every Monday morning, followed by a cold lunch from the remainder of the Sunday joint.

The Wicker Congregational Church seemed to be very large. I remember attending my first service there and being intrigued by the choir. They sat at the front of the church, very high up and facing the congregation and consisted entirely of women in enormous hats. They always sang an anthem of some sort and my Dad used to say

"The choir will now render the Anthem"

And render it they did! Every time! I wonder sometimes if he used to use that verb with tongue in cheek, or if it was an innocent expression not to be misinterpreted by the likes of me.

Andrew & Margaret, Sheffield

Tall Wee Tale

G oing to school was a whole new experience. Our house was at the top of a hill and we had to walk down to the main road and catch a tramcar to school. I'd never been on a tram before and it was great fun climbing up the stairs to travel on the top deck and look out on to the passing houses from such a high up position. It didn't take me long to realise there was a big round metal pedal on the floor of the deck where the passengers alighted which would sound out a bell if you jumped on to it, which I did every time I got off. I think it was supposed to be used by the conductress to request the driver to pull up at the next tram stop. But it supplied me with endless naughty pleasures each day on my way to school.

Because my sister Margaret was slightly older than me she went to the Junior School, whilst I was in the Infants. The school buildings were separated by quite a large playground and so during the day I was unable to see her, and I wasn't used to that, and in some ways I felt quite vulnerable and alone.

Teaching in those days was quite formal. We sat in rows in front of the teacher and concentrated on the blackboard but we also had sessions out in the playground where we could use the wooden toys on offer. Most had chipped paint and I remember the railway engine only had three wheels. When I pointed this out to the teacher she always replied, "I know Andrew, we must have it repaired."

I wondered how long it would be before a wheel was found as it had been like this since I had arrived at school!

It came as a great surprise when one day our teacher announced to us all that we had been chosen to represent the school at a Physical Education display in the city of Sheffield. I don't know how I was included in this as PE was not my best subject but on the actual day of our performance we were taken to the venue in Sheffield on a double decker bus and I found that to be an adventure in itself. We gave our performance to rapturous applause and were given a silver cup. Our teacher seemed highly delighted and was in a very chatty mood all the way home.

My gran often used to collect me from school and this particular day she was late in arriving. I'd been waiting some time with my friend Tommy Hardcastle when I told him I was bursting for a wee and so off we went to the boy's toilets which were situated in the playground. There was a six-foot wall surrounding the place where the boys had to wee and on this occasion we decided to have a little bet to see if one of us could wee over the wall.

I knew this was going to be a challenge and a half. Tommy went first but was clearly a good six inches short of the summit. As I was waiting for him to perform I had already worked out a strategy. I'd hold back until I was ready to burst and then let fire. It was a rip roaring success and Tommy was rolling about on the floor laughing his head off cheering and shouting "Big Willy, Big Willy wins"

Suddenly I heard a great screech from the other side of the wall and my gran marched round the corner holding her hat in her hands. It had come into the direct line of fire. Tommy ran off.

"You dirty little monkey," she said, "You dirty little beggar. Get yourself home this very minute. Wait till your mother hears about this. Just look at my hat."

I did look at it and nearly fell about laughing. Although, I was a bit nervous of what to expect when I got home.

I was told my behaviour was disgusting and I ought to be ashamed of myself and my gran repeated all the graphic details of my actions and added to them by displaying her hat as evidence. I went to bed in disgrace. But nevertheless I felt a certain degree of pride that I had beaten Tommy Hardcastle in the challenge. After all, to wee over a six foot wall in a perfect parabola was no mean achievement.

Andrew & Margaret, Sheffield

A School Meal Exposed

Years later when I was Head Teacher of a Primary School I remembered all of my misdoings and my own little crimes when children were sent to me.

I'd like to think I was always sympathetic to their problems but on many occasions they really made me laugh. Although I always managed to keep a straight face.

Daniel and Peter were sent to me one day by my Deputy Head. Apparently Daniel had been saying something awful about the school meal to his friend Peter and Mrs Blakey had unfortunately heard him.

"This boy has been extremely rude and he has been using bad language as well."

Daniel looked a bit sheepish but his friend looked quite pleased that Daniel was getting into trouble.

Textured vegetable protein had just been added to school meals and our cook that day had made a pie of it. Nothing had been added to it and nothing taken away and I must admit it did taste rather bland.

Eventually I wandered over to the two boys and asked them to explain what was going on between them. They were very quiet but eventually Peter said that Daniel had said a swear word about his dinner.

Daniel looked horrified. "I didn't Mr Woodhouse, I never did, I didn't honest."

"He did," chimed in Peter, "he did."

"No, I didn't!"

"You did."

Eventually, I asked Peter what Daniel had said.

"Mr Woodhouse, he said that his dinner was shit,"

"What?" I stood back in disbelief.

"Yes, Mr Woodhouse. "He said it was shit." Daniel couldn't believe his ears as he heard the dreaded word blurted out once again.

"I didn't, I didn't, Mr. Woodhouse, I didn't, I said it was bloody lovely. I said it was bloody lovely."

"Go back to your places," I said "and stop being such naughty boys."

"Daniel, you come here for a moment. Now what do you say?"

"I'm sorry Mr Woodhouse and I won't do it again."

"I should think not. I don't know where you pick up such dreadful language. You don't hear it at school."

"I know," he said. "It's my Uncle George, he's a lorry driver!"

Funny Games

I'll always remember the two girls who were sent to me by Mrs Bland when she'd been on duty in the playground. Mrs Bland had quite an intense approach to teaching in the classroom and she was the type of person who looked into everything with a scrutinizing eye. She frequently made more of things than was necessary and she was very much into psychology. I always imagined, given the chance, she would refer anyone for psychological or psychiatric help even if they had only tripped over a PE mat.

"Mr Woodhouse. You must speak to these two girls. Fiona has been extremely rude to Daphne and embarrassed her beyond measure. I don't know what's been going on, but look how red with embarrassment she is."

I noticed that Daphne was a bit red, but Fiona looked more uncomfortable and embarrassed.

Mrs Bland disappeared and the two girls stood next to each other waiting to see what I was going to say.

"Well Fiona, what's been going on and what have you done to Daphne that was so rude?"

"Daphne, I presume Fiona was rude to you when you were out on the playground?"

"Yes, Mr Woodhouse, she was."

"Well, what happened?"

No reply!

"Fiona, what happened?"

Fiona looked at the floor and didn't reply. I was getting a bit impatient and it probably showed.

"What were you doing Fiona?"

"We were playing a game"

"A game? What sort of game?"

"Well, you take a piece of paper and fold it up and then you number it and you have to pick a number."

And?"

"Well when you pick a number there's a question behind it and then you have to read the question. Then you have to pick another number and read out the answer."

"Is that all," I said, "is that it?"

"Yes Mr Woodhouse that's all it was, honest."

"Well what was the question?"

Fiona continued to looked at the floor as though she needed a hole to appear and swallow her up. Daphne was looking the other way.

"What was the question?"

Fiona whispered something and made a few unintelligible noises.

"Oh for heaven's sake, what…was…the…question?"

In a slightly more audible whisper Fiona said,

"What would you do if you saw your boyfriend's willy?"

"Oh my goodness," I said and shook my head from side to side to register my disbelief at such a question. But of course by now I was fascinated to know the answer.

"Well," I said in a tone that indicated you might as well confess all now.

"Well what on earth was the answer?"

Another inaudible whisper followed. I was dying to hear the answer.

"What was the answer?"

"Bite it off!"

With that and after a little chastisement I returned them to their teacher.

Later, Mrs Bland asked me if I had found out the reason why Fiona had been so embarrassed.

"Yes," I said. "Just hope and pray that Daphne never sees her boyfriend's willy."

The Civic Service

The hymns at the Wicker Congregational Church were always a delight because they were played by a very competent musician on the most magnificent organ I'd ever heard. It was made up of some outstanding pipe work and roused the congregation to really praise the Lord. It seemed to fulfil the words of Psalm 150, "Praise him with trumpet sound, praise him with strings and pipe." This, I thought was the instrument for me and I was overjoyed when my father took me up to the organ loft and after chatting to the organist I was allowed to have a go on the keys and try out a few stops. From then on I was determined to learn to read music and become an organist myself. Years later my desire was fulfilled and I began to play the organ for my father in some of his churches.

However, my enthusiasm really did get the better of me on one occasion. I'd been organist at the local parish church in a large market town in North Yorkshire for some years and had always attempted to lighten services by playing relevant well known pieces of music and songs we could use for worship. I also chose hymns for the choir that bounced along and made for a happy experience.

We were preparing for what was to be a well-attended Civic Service one Sunday morning and most of the towns organisations were to be there. The Mayor and Counsellors, The British Legion, scouts and guides and representatives of the town's commerce, schools and health workers were all to attend as well as our usual congregation. The service was to begin with the National Anthem. This I thought was a great opportunity to show my real skill on the organ. The Friday night before the service I was at the organ practicing the music and decided to introduce the National Anthem with a magnificent drum roll and so I sorted this out on the pedals. I knew this had not been accomplished before. This was a first and everyone would surely be impressed. The drum roll I had ready, sounded brilliant.

Sunday morning arrived and the church filled with the dignitaries and various community groups and the vicar welcomed all and sundry. I was ready at the organ and when we were told to stand for the singing of the National Anthem my feet felt for the pedals and I sounded forth my drum roll. To this day I still re-live the horror of realising I had opened out the wrong stops and my carefully prepared introduction to the Nation's Anthem sounded dreadful. It was like the uncontrollable flatulence of a herd of large elephants that filled and echoed and re-echoed around the church building. I played on but no one sang and as I looked around it seemed that the whole of the assembled congregation were in fits of laughter.

At that moment I wished for a hole in which to hide. The vicar was a bit taken aback. But he just took off his spectacles and said, "I think we'll try that again." And so we did, but this time without a drum roll. It's not surprising therefore that ever since that unfortunate event whenever I hear or sing The National Anthem I can't help a little giggle recalling the tribe of flatulating elephants at that Civic Service.

A Concert Debut

Sometimes visiting musicians performed at the Wicker Congregational Church and their concerts were usually a pleasure to hear. I felt quite an affinity to any brass player as their resounding instruments seemed to lift me to heights unknown.

Whilst serving as church organist at the local parish church I'd become very close friends with Eric who sang in the choir. Now Eric could play the trumpet really well, so we eventually teamed up and he used to play for some of the hymns, especially at Easter. I think the congregation thought we had installed a special trumpet stop.

He also brought it along to our carol singing and as we travelled from venue to venue played the Post Horn Gallop through the car window, much to everyone's rapturous delight!

Eric and I were invited to perform at a posh concert to be held for a charitable trust at a very old hall set in extensive parkland. Some of the top musicians of the area were to be there including the choir of the teacher training college.

Tickets were expensive and it was hinted that the audience were very well to do! Eric didn't want to do it at first but when I said it was for charity he relented and agreed and so we selected a simple piece for piano and trumpet by Mozart.

We kept meaning to practise but by the time we did the concert loomed on the horizon. Dressed in our best bib and tucker we arrived at the venue.

"I'm very nervous," he said.

"Nonsense," said I. "There's nothing to be nervous about."

"On with the motley."

And we took our places in the audience until it was our turn.

We were a both a little surprised to see we had made top of the bill and were on last.

"Oh no," Eric groaned, "We'll have to sit through all the concert and listen to all those professionals before it's our turn. What am I doing here? It's going to be a disaster."

"Oh, Eric do cheer up we're going to be the star turn."

But Eric looked miserable and sat there as if under sentence.

The concert moved on and the performers played and sang their hearts out. Eventually we were announced.

"Ladies and gentlemen may I present to you two fine musicians to perform our finale. Eric on the silver trumpet and Andrew on piano as they play an extract from Concerto for trumpet and piano by Mozart."

I sat at the piano stool as Eric adjusted his music on the music stand. A nod from me and we were off and I *was* off, quite a bit off, as I played all the wrong notes in the introduction.

"I'm sorry," I said "I'm terribly sorry I'll begin again."

I did but with no better result. The third time the trumpet entered with a cough.

"Uh no," I said, we'll try again."

Plinkety plonk went the piano but it was only slightly better and so embarrassing. I waited for the trumpet. This time it gave a squeak and a phlumph.

"I can't help it," said Eric, "you put me off and now I've lost my lip."

"Lost your lip? How can you lose your lip?"

The audience were beginning to titter. I felt they weren't taking us seriously and that we were crossing the line into comedy.

A kindly gentleman said to Eric "I'll fetch you a glass of water."

"Thanks," I said "and while you're out there see if you can find Eric's lip."

More laughter. The water was downed and again the piano plinkety plonked but there was no trumpet. There was only a puffing noise and a sound like a dying cow.

"It's my fault," I said, amongst the uncontrollable laughter.

"It's my fault. The music was upside down."

I turned it over to more laughter.

"Right," I said "we'll try it once more."

I wish, how I wish, we had played it perfectly but it was absolutely dreadful. Eric was red in the face but I was now enjoying our new found fame as a comical double act and the audience believed us to be so. I shrugged my shoulders took a bow and we got a standing ovation. We were congratulated by many for bringing a finale of fun to the proceedings and were asked if we would take bookings for some forthcoming concerts. A comic act was accidentally born.

Unfortunately, Eric didn't see it as such and when I put it to him on the way home he said, "You must be joking. Never, never, never again. We got ourselves into a fine mess. In fact, don't mention it ever again. Don't even speak to me ever again."

But I did and he did. Our fame spread far and wide and what happened that night has been told and retold and will probably be remembered for ever.

Drama and Friendship

Sometimes I ponder on the words of Isaac Watts in the hymn "A thousand ages in thy sight are like an evening gone" and wonder where time has gone and were all those childhood events a dream or a reality.

Certainly, I recall my days at the Junior School in Sheffield as being very happy. The building itself was old and grey, a very soot-stained Victorian monstrosity. The windows were too high for anyone to look out of and the desks were old and well worn. We had to sit still because any shuffling about might have resulted in splinters. But it was a very happy school and my teacher Miss Lennon was a lovely caring lady who made a great impression on me and the class because of her love of teaching and the concern for all in her care.

I remember the imaginative adventures she used to take us on as she recounted the life of Alexander the Great and the story of the little boy who apparently saved thousands from a great flood by putting his finger into the side of a leaking dyke in Holland. To illustrate this story we built a dyke using matchboxes and plasticine. We had been collecting matchboxes at home and one morning my dad arrived with dozens of them that he had apparently collected from neighbours as well.

When he gave them to Miss Lennon she was really appreciative and afterwards she told me she thought I had a great Dad. That made me feel really special.

Miss Lennon was the lady who first introduced me to drama. She used to tell us lots of interesting stories including the story of The Swineherd. This story by Hans Christian Anderson tells of a poor Prince who wants to marry the Emperor's daughter and sends her two beautiful gifts, a nightingale and a rose. The Princess rejects these gifts because they are real and not artificial. She prefers mechanical gifts. The Prince disguises himself and applies for the job of swineherd at the palace. He gets the job and he then makes a musical pot. The princess wants it so much that she slogs through the mud to the swineherd's house and when he asks for ten kisses for it she reluctantly agrees and gets the pot.

Afterwards he makes a musical rattle and she gives him a hundred kisses for it. The Emperor is so disgusted with his daughter for kissing a swineherd for a toy he casts her out of the palace. The Prince then cleans himself up, puts on his royal robes and decides to reject the Princess. The Princess is left alone feeling sorry for herself.

Miss Lennon told us that we were going to enact this story as part of the school concert to be held at the end of term. Each class was to contribute to the concert. As we were going to perform The Swineherd she wanted anyone who would like to be in it to raise their hands. Now I wasn't so sure about this, but there was a very beautiful girl in our class called Wendy Ibbertson and I was quite attracted to her. I considered the fact that if I did volunteer I might even be chosen as the swineherd and if she were the princess, as she was most certainly going to be, on account of her beauty, I might, according to the story be in line for a number of kisses.

I put up my hand and our names were written down. We had to have an audition for the various parts and Miss Lennon explained what that meant. We all had a little try at acting the various characters and then she would choose who would play them.

Wendy, as expected, was chosen to be the princess and I tried so hard to act like a swineherd and then a prince. I wasn't chosen and I was so bitterly disappointed and just a bit envious of Michael Appleton who was given the part. By gum, I thought to myself, I bet I can kiss better than him any day! But it was not to be and I had to be content with being a villager.

I don't think Wendy thought a great deal of Michael and eventually Wendy and I became good friends.

Several years later, I happened to be standing on Sheffield Station, when I was travelling from Leeds to Derby by train. As I looked around at the other waiting passengers I thought I saw a lady who looked very much like Wendy. Could this be the Wendy from Junior school days? I wandered across and engaged her in conversation. I couldn't hold back for long and I asked if by any chance her name was Wendy Ibbertson. It was!

What a chance meeting. Here was the girl of my childhood dreams and she remembered me as well. We talked for a while and happily for her and rather sadly for me she told me that she was to be married the next day. So as we parted I wished her every loving wish for a happy future. I wondered if she was going to marry the Prince after all.

As the train to Derby pulled away I waved to her on the platform and I thought of the little girl I knew at school, and was grateful for having such a friend.

Miss Lennon with her class, Sheffield Primary School

Snow in Sheffield

In 1947 it snowed in Sheffield. That year it snowed across the entire country from January until March. I can recall looking out of the bay window of our house as the first flakes of snow fell on that morning in January.

At first it was a welcome sight and the white flakes transformed the worn pavements and the grey road and the smoke-stained roofs into a fairy wonderland. The snow tidied all the gardens into a uniform white magical carpet and everywhere looked clean and bright. The snow kept falling and falling.

It seemed that we may have to live in a world of snow forever. My sister and I built lots of snowmen in the back yard and up in the garden. We also threw snowballs at the visiting stray cats of which there were many. Our garden seemed to be a rendezvous for all the stray cats in the district. The garden behind the house was left empty because of this. Dad said it wasn't worth the effort of cultivating it when all his past efforts of trying to grow plants and vegetables were a waste of time because they were either dug up or peed on by all the cats. So he had acquired an allotment that was some distance up the road. In fact, it was situated in an area behind our school and quite frequently I walked there with him as he pushed his wheelbarrow along.

Gardening was out at the moment, snow clearing was in! It was quite a mammoth task each day to try to keep our paths open. The road outside of the house was blocked by snow and walking was difficult. The radio was our only means of news and the outlook was bleak. Trains, buses and all public transport including the trams were at a standstill. Sheffield like the rest of the country had ground to a halt. This went on for weeks, but we managed to walk to school.

There were narrow walkways between the high walls of snow and I found getting to school quite an adventure. We had to wear wellington boots most of the time and after walking in them every day my legs were quite chapped around my knees.

My ever considerate mother said, "Your legs are quite sore. If you don't cover them or wear something over them, they'll get worse. It's because they're cold when you're walking to school. I'll think of something." And she did!

Her solution was to send me to school wearing a pair of my sister's long Lyle stockings. I'll never understand my mother's obsession for sending me to school dressed in girls' accessories. The next morning after much protest, I was thus attired. But I felt so uneasy and so self-conscious about it all I pulled my navy blue gabardine raincoat down over my legs as I walked. I must have looked silly, trying to walk that way.

I kept my coat on as I stood in line in the playground waiting to go into class. Unfortunately, once inside, the coat had to come off and it was then that Mavis Fenshaw saw my long stockings. She nudged a few of the other girls and then the lads came over and they all started to walk about in silly ways pretending they were wearing long stockings and showing them off to each other. I was mortified by everyone's amusement but I had to wear them for the first half of the morning, at least up to midmorning break.

At playtime I ran into the washroom, sat down and took off the offending apparel! Then I dashed onto the playground and wreaked my revenge on all those who had teased me remorselessly by engaging them all in snowball fights. After that things reverted back to normal and long stockings were soon forgotten. At the end of the day, so as not to cause any trouble at home, I slipped on the long stockings and crept out of school.

"You see," said my mum, they were a good idea of mine. They've kept your legs dry and healed all that chapping on your knees. You're a good lad. Go get your tea."

So I did. The next morning we couldn't find those long Lyle stockings anywhere so I had to go to school without them. I still can't remember where I put them.

Mother

Our mother was very special to all of us. She always had time to listen to us and encourage us, and she frequently made us laugh at many of her ways. I think, looking back over the years when we were young she had her work cut out to keep an eye on us all and react with advice or justifiable rage if we behaved in a stupid way. In my case I was told to behave so frequently I was in my early teens before I realised my Christian name was not "Behave!"

Once we were being so annoying to her for some reason she grabbed a large wooden spoon and intended to use it on us, but we all ran out of the house and up the road to escape but, looking behind, she was still chasing us. All around the houses we fled.

The neighbours must have thought it an unusual sight.

We hid for hours in the attic of the house until she calmed down. As we crouched up there together we could hear her talking to Gran all about what had happened and laughing quietly in the kitchen.

My mother was good at doing different voices. She could go from shouting at us like a "fish wife" which she did with great effect when we were being a nuisance, to the charms of the upper crust that she used to impress.

On one occasion Mum was chasing us up the stairs I presume to grab one of us for being so naughty.

"You little beggars, come 'ere or I'll knock the 'livin' daylights out of yer!"

We could hardly get up the stairs for laughing. Then the telephone rang and suddenly Mum's voice changed.

"Helew? Morrison Manse hare, kin I hilp yew?

Turning to us she whispered, "Just you lot wait!" And so this was just another side to our lovely mum in action.

Sickness was to be avoided in my childhood. Mainly because remedies were not so good and apart from the common cold it often took a long time for sickness to pass. I had a severe dose of tonsillitis and my throat burned like a furnace and swallowing was dreadfully painful. I recall her watching over me by my bedside as she sat close to me in Gran's old armchair and held my hand. She never left my side. My illness seemed to rest on her shoulders and it seemed to just go on and on. The local doctor said that it would just have to run its course.

Then one night Gran came to see how I was getting on. Mum asked me to open my mouth a bit so Gran could see what Mum had seen earlier.

"Good heavens," said Gran, "his tonsils are all covered in yellow."

Mum and Gran were a bit concerned about this and I watched as they left the room and I could hear them mumbling behind the bedroom door and eventually I heard Mum say, "Alright then, I think I'll try tomorrow."

As I dozed into a sleep I wondered what it was they planned for tomorrow. I soon found out. Mid-morning Mum and Gran came up to my bedside with a little round bowl of liquid and what looked like buds of cotton wool on the end of sticks.

"Now, our Andrew," said Mum, "I'm going to get rid of all that nasty yellow stuff and get that throat of yours better. I'm fed up with it taking so long to clear."

Now Mum had always considered herself as a bit of a medic when it came to general complaints. This time I think she brought Gran along as either an assistant or to make sure she wasn't going to kill me with her treatment. Following her instructions, I lay there with my mouth wide open and my head right back and she seemed to be dabbing my tonsils with a damp cotton bud.

"You're shifting them, our Elsie," Gran reported." You're shifting the lot."

The whole procedure was painless, although my throat was still sore and when she had finished her minor operation I gargled with some warm water and was allowed to doze off again. Mum and Gran seemed to be pleased with their handiwork and so was I when a couple of days later, my throat was cured.

After this I went with Mum to have it all checked by the doctor. The doctor seemed to be a bit annoyed with my mum. She castigated her for even attempting to clean up my tonsils. She said that it was most dangerous and risky and told Mum never to attempt to try anything like that again. I was listening to all this and I thought how ungrateful of her to go on at my mum like that. After all, she'd cured me and if I'd waited as the doctor advised for it to clear up of its own accord I'd still be waiting in agony.

As we walked home I could see Mum was a bit upset and at the same time cross. I took hold of her hand and looked up to her face and told her she was magnificent, just magnificent and the best Mum in the whole world. And as we walked further she began to smile again, and I said "Thank you Mum, thank you."

Most of the houses we lived in had a cellar and a pantry. The pantry was usually just above the cellar and so made a cool place to store food and the bottles of full cream milk. It was also an ideal place in which to store mother's collection of cures for any ailments that came along. Amongst them were the usual Syrup of Figs, Witch Hazel and something called Kaolin.

She had cures for poorly eyes, noses, aching limbs, feet and headaches. In fact, remedies for all complaints. But the day she discovered "Fennings Fever Cure" was the worst day of her medical acquisitions. She considered this medicine to be the all-round cure and preventative, as stated on the bottle label. For influenza, colds, bowel complaints, griping pains and diarrhoea, as well as anything else.

Every day we had to drink an egg cupful, but it was absolutely dreadful and was real torture. It set your teeth on edge and made you shudder. It seemed to attack your tongue and it felt as though all the enamel had been stripped from your teeth. This was no wonder, as in later life I discovered that it contained diluted nitric acid.

We hung around for ages holding the egg cups. I was thinking that perhaps having the ailments was less traumatic.

Eventually we managed to get the poison down holding our noses and shutting our eyes, but it was an effort.

I do remember well that once my brother David decided that he'd had enough of it all, when our mum had gone out of the room, he poured his into a plant pot.

When Mum came back in she looked at my sister and I and said, "Oh, do get a move on. David managed to get his down quickly. Why can't you do the same?"

Margaret and I said nothing, but I was really mad with my brother David that day as he stood behind our mum with a great big grin on his face.

Throughout her life she gathered friends like a magnet, and there were many aspects of her life we didn't know about until later in life. During her lifetime she had apparently been manager of a number of businesses including the local Co-op and had been guest speaker at several local organisations in the community. Sometimes she preached at the church and was always well received. I heard her once and couldn't believe that she was our mum. She took on the mantle of a minister very well indeed.

We all felt that when her life ended she would be welcomed into heaven and the moderator of The Congregational Church, who presided over her funeral, echoed our thoughts.

Afterwards, I felt a need to record my own thoughts about the act of celebration of her life in verse and thus I wrote:

Scattered Soil

I felt her breath even closer
Than the sweet peas I dropped upon her coffin
Now resting within the earth.
These were her flowers and I brought them
From her garden. She blushed with colour.
Without her, the seasons will melt into one
And become, an adjacent Trinity.
The earth that I now scatter upon her
Was once her foothold.
And infinitely sure
She walked upon it
Until infinity
Drew in her scent
And floundered
For she was lovely.
And when the angels welcome, or whoever
Comes to greet,
May they welcome in
A guardian.
Who will lead the apostles
To find the earth and goodness
Closer than the darkness
Of scattered soil?

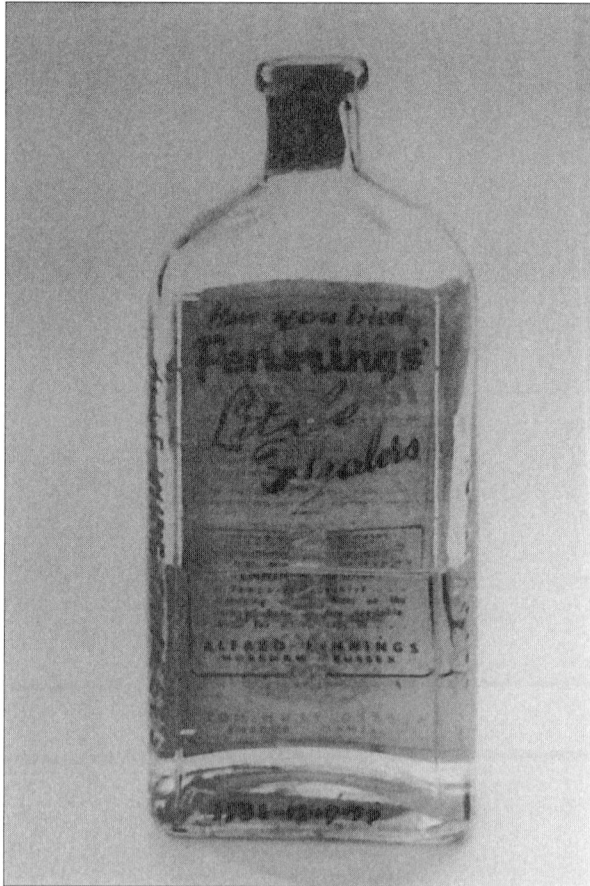

Fenning Fever Cure

Ear Ache and Blakey's Chalet

The snow passed and soon the first spring blossom could be seen on the bare trees of winter in Abbeyfield Park. We often visited this park as the gardens were very attractive. But, there was an area at the lower end by the lake where the swings were situated that was very gloomy which we avoided. We pretended that there were goblins and nasty creatures down there.

At the top end of the park there were lovely gardens and it was here where most people walked and took in the scents of the flowers.

It was on a visit that I first began to sense a pain in my right ear. It gradually became almost unbearable and any appreciation for the lovely flowers and plants left me completely, as I struggled to contain the agony of my earache.

I was taken swiftly home and my mother arranged to take me to see Doctor Slade. He diagnosed a severe infection and gave my mum some ear drops to administer. The infection became much worse and at one point the doctor was attending every other day. My pain was excruciating and my ear was now producing a lot of puss. Medication in those days was fairly limited and I remember my mum wrapping cotton wool around the end of a medium sized knitting needle and carefully inserting it into my ear to collect and soak up any discharge. The pain was agonising and to recall it even now is painful.

I often fought off the needle and sometimes my dad held my head so my mum could perform her painful duty. After what seemed to be many painful weeks she attained her goal and cured me. And what a relief that was. But having been ill for such a long time and as my ear was still sensitive I found it difficult to keep my balance when I walked. Because of this it was decided that I needed a holiday and so it was we left home to take up residence for a week in Mr and Mrs Blakey's chalet.

Falling Around

Mr and Mrs Blakey were the caretakers at The Congregational Church and they offered my dad their chalet for a week. The chalet was on a farm in Derbyshire in the Peak District. He gratefully accepted and one sunny spring day we travelled by train to our destination and having arrived, asked the porter on the railway platform the way to the farm. After a great deal of conversation and direction giving we set off.

It was a long way, further than we expected, but eventually after following a few footpaths and crossing a few fields we could see the farm in the distance. It was a long way to carry our bags and luggage. Fortunately, because of my inability to keep a true balance, following my ear infection, I was not expected to lend a hand and I made sure of this by letting my legs wobble a bit extra now and again.

We were met by a very friendly farmer and his wife and they pointed the way to the chalet. It was behind the farmhouse and it was perched on the top of a steep hill. Although it was supposed to be a chalet it looked to me more like a long narrow box and it didn't look very safe there, I thought, perched on the top and on the edge of that hill.

We all bundled inside relieved to have made the journey and Mum and Gran were grateful for the food and provisions the farmer's wife had provided.

That night it rained hard and the roof leaked, so we had to find buckets to put under the drips. I was in a bed next to my sister Margaret. She had brought a rag doll with a pot head with her called Jemima and I noticed she had it in bed with her. A bit sloppy, that, I thought. One night she accidentally left the doll outside and it rained again all night. In the morning when she went to get her doll it was wet through.

"O dear," I said, "looks as though Jemima will die of pneumonia now." She wasn't very pleased but Mum soon had the doll dried out and all was well again.

That was more than could be said of my little escapade. It was Sunday morning. Dad had left us the day before to return home overnight so that he could take the services that Sunday morning at the Wicker Church. He was returning tonight and had promised to bring Margaret and me a present. It was strange not to have Dad with us but we passed our time pleasantly enough during the day.

At the bottom of the hill from the chalet there was a stream and Margaret and myself paddled about and built dams for most of the morning. Then after lunch my mum decided we ought to go for a walk. Mum's walks were exceptional. She had no idea where she intended to go and just set off. We ended most walks by getting completely lost and usually at a dead end. Every time it was the same and every time she came out with the same catch phrase, "I think I know a short cut back." At which we all used to fall about laughing. We made it back eventually and today was no exception. A cup of tea was on offer but I'd noticed that Margaret had disappeared.

"Where's Margaret gone?" I asked.

"She's gone to see the cows being milked. The farmer asked if she would like to pop round and have a look."

"Have a look?" I said, "Have a look? I'd like to have a look as well."

And I jumped up and made for the door.

"Wait!" cried Mum, "it's beginning to rain. Put your mac on if you're going out."

I flung my mac on as fast as I could and flew out of the door in case I was going to miss anything. I was a bit cross that I hadn't been invited and ran as fast as I could towards the dairy. The farmer turned to look as I sped through the door.

"Ey up," he said, "What we got 'ere?"

I was travelling so fast, I couldn't stop. I caught sight of my sister standing there open mouthed as I shot past her, slipped on the floor and slid all the way along through all the cow muck and wee.

"Well now, what HAVE we got 'ere?" said the farmer as I tried to get up and slipped again into the cow dung.

"O lawd," I said, "O lawd."

"What are you trying to do?" asked my sister, who couldn't believe her eyes.

"Why, O why does it always happen to me?" I cried.

"Oh dear," said the farmer, "I think you'd better be getting back home and get cleaned up."

"Hang on." he said and he grabbed a handful of dry hay and tried to wipe some of the muck from my mac. My other clothing and my knees were well covered as well. He took off his hat and scratched his head.

"You'd best be getting back to thee mam."

Taking his advice, I turned and made a very undignified exit from the dairy closely followed by my sister who was holding her nose.

"Andrew! Andrew! What on earth have you been doing now? Don't come in here. Stay where you are. Give me your coat. Right, now carefully take off anything that has any cow muck on it."

"Come and look at this mother," she said to Gran and Gran came.

"What next," she said, "what on earth has he been doing now?"

I felt like saying, "Well actually Gran I thought I'd give all the cows permission to poo on me and so I stood behind them." But I didn't and having done what my mum had instructed me to do I now stood there naked.

"I'll have to take all these clothes in and try to give them a good wash." she said.

"I'll give you a hand," said Gran.

Whilst they were dealing with my smelly clothes I had to have a bath. I must say I felt a lot better when I put on some fresh clothes.

"That's better. You didn't half pong!" Margaret said.

My washed attire was hung to dry around the small fire on a wooden clothes horse.

"I hope we can get all this cleared up before your Dad comes back. He won't want to be coming in to all this washing on a Sunday," said Mum.

"It won't take long," said Gran and it didn't. It was all eventually folded up and put in a washing basket in the bathroom.

"I think we'll have our tea," Mum said, "as your Dad won't be home until later on. He can have his when he arrives."

So tea was duly prepared and enjoyed and then we waited for Dad.

There wasn't much to entertain us in the evening, so we had to be content with listening to a crackly radio and the strains of The Palm Court Orchestra. We sat looking out of the window for what seemed ages looking for any signs of Dad returning. Then he came into sight. We could see him down the valley walking towards us and we were all happy to see him.

"Here he comes."

We followed his journey up the hill and when he was only a short distance away Margaret and I ran to greet him. He was pleased to see us and once inside Mum gave him a big kiss and I looked away. But then he opened his brief case and asked if we had been good children.

"Yes we have." I said.

Mum was about to say something but didn't. Then Dad gave us the little presents he said he was going to bring back for us. Margaret had a new doll and I was given two little racing cars. One red and one green. What fabulous presents.

Dad said he'd had a good trip and was looking forward to the next few days at Blakey's Chalet. He disappeared into his bedroom and came out later dressed for the country.

"You look the part now Dad." I said.

As he sat down at the table to have his tea he sniffed, "Does it smell like cows in here to you?"

Aberfield Park, Sheffield

I Don't Believe in Fairies

Iris Hoyes was probably my first encounter with a bully. She was in the top class of the Junior School and she was a very large girl. She wore grey and that made her all the more intimidating. Her grey blouse was covered by a grey woollen pullover and her grey skirt almost touched her grey socks that she allowed to fall to her ankles and I remember she wore large black leather boots that had metal studs on the soles and heels. She tormented the younger children at every opportunity and today it was the turn of my sister and I.

I'd just lost my first tooth and Margaret had told me all about the tooth fairy. If I put the tooth under my pillow that night, the tooth fairy would collect it and leave me a sixpence. That sounded like a good idea so I kept it wrapped in an old handkerchief in the pocket of my trousers all day for safety. At the end of the school day, Margaret, who was in a higher class than myself waited for me at the school gate. Beside her was Iris Hoyes.

"You're daft," she said, "if you believe in that barmy story about the tooth fairy."

I think she must have heard that I had lost a tooth.

"I don't believe in fairies. I don't believe in fairies." she kept on chanting,

"I don't believe in fairies!"

It seemed like she went on forever. Then suddenly my sister burst out crying.

"What's the matter?" I asked.

"Well every time she says I don't believe in fairies a fairy dies."

"You daft thing," said Iris and she began to say it even more. So my sister and I ran off and on the way home we kept singing, "We believe in fairies" for every time you say that, a fairy is born and so together we helped to increase the fairy population.

That night I had my belief confirmed as the following morning I found a bright new sixpence under my pillow. I still tell my children about the tooth fairy and will tell my grandchildren but not about Iris Hoyes who said she didn't believe.

I bumped into her a number of years later. She was working at a checkout in a supermarket. In many ways she had changed and it was a pleasant meeting. As we were talking her son came along. He was tall with long shoulder length hair, ear rings, camel hair waistcoat and day glow jeans.

"Just look at him," she said, "He looks a right fairy!"

Wash Day

Wash day seemed a less dramatic day in spring and summer when wet clothes could be dried on a line outside, but when days began to darken in winter, wash day became formidable.

Our house in Sheffield had a fairly large kitchen with a black leaded fire range and boiler and beyond the kitchen there was a scullery.

It had been raining throughout one of these winter nights and it was still dark and pouring with rain when my sister and I walked into our kitchen one Monday morning for some breakfast.

My gran was leaning over the range poking the fire and stirring the embers, making the fire into a furnace as sparks flew like stars and fireworks up the black sooty chimney. Pans of many sizes and shapes boiled and bubbled on the red hot hob and steam spluttered and flew out of the pans to fill the room with a dense fog. Beyond in the scullery we could see the great dolly tubs. From them also issued steam and suds.

Dad was frantically pummeling what appeared to be clothes with a poggle stick whilst Mum was pulling out various pieces of wet clothing to put through a mangle. The whole of the kitchen and scullery were full of steam and soapy smells. It was almost impossible to see across the room through the fog made by all of the steam.

"Any chance of some breakfast yet?" I asked, more in hope than expectation.

"You'll have to see to yourselves today," said Gran, "you can see we're busy. Just get some cornflakes for now."

"I feel as though I'm standing in the engine room of the Titanic," I said. "We seem to be all letting off steam today, hey?"

"You'll be letting off steam in a minute," Dad bellowed from the scullery, "if you don't be quiet and get your breakfast. You can see we're all busy."

I wasn't going to upset him today, so I didn't reply but I wondered why he had a tea cosy on his head.

My father had some strange ways. Apart from being attracted to tea cosies he often wore an apron around the house especially on wash days. I suppose it was for protection, but as he was wearing his old clothes anyway, I couldn't see the point.

On Sundays he was always very smartly dressed and my mum said once that someone in the church congregation had even remarked on the pure whiteness of his handkerchiefs. She was very proud of that. I must say I preferred to see Dad dressed smartly, but this seemed to be only when he was going out. This was because he had this strange habit of changing into his old tatty clothes, as soon as he was indoors. He used to tell me that changing into old clothes preserved his best outfits and what he saved in that expense, he could spend elsewhere. However, he never seemed to spend anything elsewhere, or anywhere else for that matter. Dad just never seemed to spend!

In the winter months he was often to be seen wearing a tea cosy on his head and carrying a hot water bottle. I suppose he was trying to save fuel. Sometimes I felt sorry for him for it was often very cold in his study where he worked, but we were fortunate as we could huddle around the fire in the kitchen.

This wash day was going very well, with copious amounts of steam. The whole kitchen reeked of washing powder and soap. The boiler in the scullery had reached boiling point and Dad was now filling buckets of hot water to empty into the dolly tubs. There was non-stop activity in progress and although my sister tried to help a bit I kept out of the way. I knew from bitter experience that if anything happened to go wrong it would be my fault. I sat in the corner and looked through the Beano, I had read it several times already, but couldn't think of anything else to do.

Mid-morning arrived and all activity stopped apart from the continuous bubbling of the boiler in the scullery.

"Right," said Dad, "let's have a break. Coffee time."

In anticipation Gran had already put out some cups, a bottle of milk and a bowl of sugar on the kitchen table.

Mum said, "Nay, I think we'll pour the milk into a milk jug. We're not working in a factory."

It seemed that way to me too but I kept quiet. Maybe not a factory but certainly a laundry.

The milk was boiled and the bottle of coffee came out of the cupboard. I always thought it was a strange tasting substance and smelt of liquorice. It was called Camp coffee and came in a tall thin brown bottle. It was only years later when I had my first taste of 'real' coffee that I discovered what it *should* taste like. I didn't like this Camp coffee but was expected to drink it. After my first sip I couldn't help but say "Yup", and was told to stop being silly.

"I'll give you "Yup" if you say that again." Dad said.

So, I didn't and I wondered why Dad kept repeating everything I said. I drank it and ran outside into the backyard in the pouring rain and was sick.

I decided to keep a very low profile after that. But some good came out of it, I wasn't given any more of it to drink. As the morning rolled on, the washing came to an end and all the tubs and pans were put away until the following week. The boiler was emptied and the mangle wiped down and there was a general tidy up. But, all was not over as now there was a great pile of damp and wet clothes to get dried. Gran was back at the fire again poking the embers and putting on more coal. The heat was soon almost unbearable and I had to take off my pullover.

"You can put that back on." said Dad. "You'll be sick again if you take that off!"

I just thought I'd feel more sick if I kept it on, but back on it went. Anything for a bit of peace.

Soon the kitchen looked like an Arabian tent. Damp clothes hung down from the ceiling from a great long pulley and clothes horses were festooned with all sorts of attire and even more steam rose into the air. So it remained until every last piece of clothing was dry and fit for the ironing board.

Mondays were hard work. It was also a custom that Monday dinner times consisted of the left-overs from Sunday. We had cold meat, usually beef and we had some sort of pickle with it. I enjoyed that and in some ways it made up for all the horrors of a washday.

Later that day I thought it would have been very funny if we had any visitors to our house and they'd seen all this array of steaming shirts, vests, socks, underpants and knickers.

I was already in bother again because there was a line up of three enormous pink bloomers hanging down from the ceiling all steaming away and I got the giggles. My sister told me to behave and not to say anything, because they belonged to Gran.

"Cor," I thought to myself, "I'm glad they don't belong to Mum." I just couldn't stop laughing.

"It must have taken a lot of washing powder to sort them out Gran."

"I'll sort you out in a minute my lad," Dad growled.

There he goes again, I thought, repeating everything I say.

"Don't be so silly our Andrew," Mum said. She always called me "our" Andrew when she was being mad with me.

"You wait," she said, "when you get old you might want something like that to keep you warm in the winter."

Blimey, I thought. I could pass myself off as a very plausible Aladdin in a big pair of knickers like these. They would make an excellent pair of pantaloons.

And so the day eventually came to an end and all the clothes were dry. It seemed we had all survived the day. But we had it all to look forward to again the following week.

Dad read my sister Margaret and myself a bedtime story that night. It was my sister's turn to choose which one.

"Dad can we have Amelia Ann's Washing Day please?"

"Course you can," said Dad.

I was about to say,

"Oh flippin heck!" but I didn't.

Mum & Dad

Brownies

There was a large group of young men who used to meet occasionally at The Wicker Congregational Church. They dressed in bluish uniforms and they paraded in formation behind a band of drummers and bugle players. I was told they were called The Boys Brigade and they marched through the streets around the church playing music before attending the service and then marched back around the streets afterwards. Dad used to go with them and sometimes he used to take me with him. I enjoyed all the music and marching along to the drum beat. One day I said to my mum that I fancied a uniform like the one The Boys Brigade wore and I wished I was in something like that.

"You're too young," she said, "but I have an idea you might like."

Mum's ideas were not always good ideas and I just wondered what she had in mind. I soon found out.

One Sunday shortly after that, we had a lady for lunch who I had not met before. Strangely she was introduced as Auntie Rene. She wasn't very tall and didn't look as though she was a part of our family. I think I'd seen her at the church talking to my mum after the service. She said that she ran a group at the church called the Brownies and she had already invited my sister Margaret to go along and join them and Margaret said she would and she looked forward to it. Now at the time I had no idea what the Brownies were and when Mum said she would get Margaret a uniform my ears pricked up. A uniform? If they wore a uniform, I might be interested myself! Before I could say anything Mum said she had asked Auntie Rene if I could go along with Margaret and Rene had agreed but I had to behave well.

"Fair enough." I said, and that night I went to bed happy, looking forward to a new adventure with the "Brownie Club". I didn't have to wait long.

One evening soon after Rene's visit my sister and I arrived at the church and we were met by a robust and rotund girl called Mavis Pemberton who escorted us around the back of the church to the school room. Then quite suddenly this girl who had introduced herself simply disappeared. I hadn't realised it at the time but she had darted off to tell all her female friends that a stupid boy had arrived. Rene came to the door and took us into the room.

This is strange, it's full of girls. I thought. It was.

I was the only boy there, but I said nothing. This might be to my advantage! We were asked to form a circle and when we had made this, I asked where the boys were. This was greeted by silly giggles from all the girls.

"The Brownies are a girls group Andrew," said Rene, "but you're very welcome to come along with your sister, if you wish."

I wasn't very happy and although I had earlier hoped for a splendid uniform, a brown dress and yellow toggle hardly fitted the bill. Why my mum sent me along here knowing it was for girls I'll never know to this day. As I say she had some strange ideas sometimes. I can only imagine that she probably thought it would keep me occupied for a while and would give her a bit of peace.

I certainly didn't go back and I was really mad with Mum for even thinking I'd enjoy the Brownies. Occasionally I had to go along with Margaret when Mum and Dad had to go out and hadn't a baby sitter and so at those times I was a bit of a rebel and made a nuisance of myself by making silly comments and I remember plunging the room into darkness once by turning the lights off. I wasn't welcome after that, but I wasn't sorry. Anyway, strangely enough I still remember the Brownie promise after all these years:

I promise that I will do my best
To do my duty to God
To serve the King (as it was then) and my country
To help other people
And to keep the Brownie Guide Law.

Many years later when I used to conduct the Remembrance Service at The Cenotaph and all the organisations were gathered together, I sometimes glanced across to the Brownies and thought, "I bet you would never guess that once upon a time, I've been one too!"

I found out later that originally the girls were called Rosebuds, but were renamed by Olive Baden-Powell after they said they were not happy with that name and became the Brownies. Their name comes from the story The Brownies by Juliana Horatia Ewing, written in 1870 in which two children Tommy and Betty learn that children can be helpful or lazy boggarts. I believe I must be a boggart!

Boggart

I believe my initial career as a boggart began the day I was sent off to boarding school. For some time now there had been lots of activity centred on myself and I had been fitted out with countless new shirts and a new herring bone suit and lots of other clothes so that I'd have much to wear, including a new football kit and new boots and I hated football! I felt as though I was being given my marching orders, but I think Mum and Dad thought it would be good for me and after all David, my brother was already there and would be able to watch over me. It was hoped I'd get a good education and it would make a man of me.

I was not quite eight years old when I left the warmth and jollity of home life and found myself as a new boy on the entrance steps of Silcoates School surrounded by most of the other boys who had gathered there. I was now called Woodhouse minor and as my brother David was older he was called Woodhouse major.

One of the big boys came over and said, "I say Woodhouse major, is this your brother?"

David said, "Yes it is."

"Well Woodhouse minor, have you got a girlfriend?"

I couldn't think what to say so I bleated out, "Yes, I think so."

"You think so? I say, what's her name then?"

I just couldn't think of anybody apart from my dear friend Wendy. So I said, "Wendy."

Then it all started. "I say chaps, Woodhouse minor has a girlfriend would you believe and her name's Wendy. From henceforth we will call you Wendy!"

So this was my initial brief meeting with the inmates that sealed my fate to be referred to as Wendy for a considerable time.

"You ought not to have said anything." David said.

But it was all a bit strange to me and after all I was still only seven.

I found my time here very stressful and was home sick on several occasions. I looked forward to the holidays, especially Christmas and the long summer breaks. We often visited Silverdale in Lancashire. We went as a family and stayed in a boarding house run by two elderly and very kind natured ladies. Silverdale was not really a seaside resort, there was no beach as such, only vast stretches of green grasses and muddy water channels. Most of the holiday was spent walking and picnicking. We walked to most of the beauty spots, including Jenny Brown's Point, Arnside Knott and the Pepperpot. We managed all this walking carrying huge bags containing the picnic food and an assortment of pullovers and coats in case it rained. Days were long and unhurried and I enjoyed us being all together as a family. Looking back maybe I ought to have appreciated them more at the time.

At night in bed I was quite frequently upset and tearful knowing that this would not last forever and I'd have to leave all this again on returning to school. I tried to be brave about it but was not much of a hero.

On holiday Dad surprised us all by saying we were to leave Sheffield and move on to a new church at Pontefract. Mum and Dad would move during term time and Gran would stay at Brimington with her sister Clara until all was sorted. We were to live in Pontefract and my brother and I arrived at our new address shortly after the "settling in" had taken place. It was a modest small three bedroomed house with a kitchen that had a good fireplace with a back boiler, and that suited Gran who always enjoyed stoking up the fire. There was a small conservatory and a good long garden. It was cosy and in the evenings we sat round the fire in the dining room and listened to our old black Murphy radio. Dad seemed happy and Mum seemed happy that he was. I tried to look cheerful but I was still worried that this would not last for long.

Once my brother David was poorly and had to stay at home at the start of term and so I was to return to school on my own. I was really upset at the thought of this. It was a Sunday evening and the whole school was in the chapel. I was sitting on the front row and my thoughts were elsewhere at home. I was wondering what was happening there.

Escape from School

The Headmaster at the time had a strange way of peering at everyone. He used to screw up his eyes as though he couldn't see very well and peer at you intensely. He kept peering like this at me and I wondered if he could read my thoughts. If he could he would have heard my brain saying "I've got to get out of here." But how?

After chapel we usually went to the locker room to change our shoes to slippers and then to the dining hall for a slice of bread and margarine and a glass of pasteurised milk.

I was wondering how on earth I could manage to slip by all the prefects on duty before bedtime roll call was made. I knew that once I was out I could catch a bus home and would pay my fare out of the five shillings I still had in my pocket that my dad had given me to bank next day with the form teacher as pocket money. So I thought of a plan of escape and put it carefully into practice.

When we went towards the locker room I sauntered past and wandered nonchalantly down the corridor and hid for a moment under a bench in the adjacent woodwork room. I waited until there was silence in the locker room and tried the door from the woodwork room to the outside. It was open! Oh joy! But, I had to be careful not to be seen. The door opened onto the rear of the school. There was a footpath leading left that went around to the front of the building and another wound its way along a grass field and tennis courts to temporary wooden classrooms. There was another track on the far left of the grass field that ran along a hedge bottom. This was for me. So crouching low I made for this and decided to scramble through the hedge to the other side so that I'd have more cover. I wasn't discovered so still bending low I made it to the corner of the field and followed along left, but still inside the field behind the hedge, and eventually came to the edge of the church graveyard.

Suddenly I heard voices and crawling into the hedge again kept very still. To be discovered now would be a tragedy. The voices and people drifted away and very carefully and gingerly I shuffled out of my hiding place. I had to make a decision. Do I risk going out onto the road on the other side of this hedge? I knew this road went straight down a hill, just a short distance to a bus stop. I knew that was the quickest route but if I went out there into the open I may be easily spotted so I decided to creep along through the churchyard between the gravestones which I found a bit spooky, and make my way to the next bus stop, which I did. I waited behind a wall until the bus came and I climbed aboard. I sat upstairs on the back seat and kept my head down, paid my fare and like Toad of The Wind in the Willows, felt as happy as he when he made his escape from prison. I soon arrived at the bus station and fortunately and as luck would have it a bus to take me home awaited and as I climbed aboard it moved off. Oh Joy, I think I've made it!

I was beginning to feel a bit tired and as I felt safe now from any pursuers I began to doze.

"Terminus!" shouted the conductor and so it was.

I leaped off the bus and made the long walk up the hill to our house. After what seemed a lifetime I stood in front of our door and rang the bell. When Gran opened it I just said, "I've come home."

"Well you'd better come in then," she said

"Well, I don't know," said Gran. "What we goin' to do with you? How did you manage to get all this way on your own? Your Mum and Dad are out at a meeting. I don't know what they're going to say when they get home."

Margaret my sister seemed to be quite interested in my exploits and I had to go over my escape details several times, and each time with more drama and apprehension to satisfy her curiosity. Meanwhile my brother David who always did have a serious streak was a bit disgusted with me and I suspect he thought I was a bit of a stupid person running away like that.

"You stupid boy," he said, "don't you realise what you've done? When you go back to school you will be watched like a hawk. Your life will not be your own."

My life never felt as though it ever was my own at this school anyway. But how comforting to be home and secure again. I'd made it!

Gran and my sister made me a bit of supper and then Gran thought it best if I went off to bed before Mum and Dad came home. She tucked me up in my cosy little bed and my sister slept next to me in the other single bed. I faintly remember my dad giving me a kiss goodnight and in my sad little way after all I had done I said thank you to my friend God for keeping me safe.

These memories remain so richly in my mind and I'm thankful for the love I was given at home and the need to get back into that love, even today.

I was surprised to wake up at home in my own bed and as I lay there remembering my night time escape that brought me here, I had to pinch myself to make sure it was true and not a dream.

Returned to School

Breakfast was a quiet affair and my brother David kept up his concern for what I had done.

"You'll always be watched now! Everyone will keep an eye on you in case you try to do another runner!"

Dad had rung the school the night before and said he would ring again to see what he ought to do.

Mum said "You can come with me this morning, but your Dad will have to take you back to school later today."

So off we went together to the shops and she bought me a little wind-up bus. I thought this was very appropriate, but I don't expect it would have occurred to her that it was a symbol of my adventurous escape. We returned home and after lunch goodbyes were said once again and Dad and I travelled back to school. How unhappy I felt. After all my efforts to escape I was now returned and my freedom curtailed.

We were met at the gate by one of the Masters and taken to meet the Headmaster in his room. Dad was ages as I waited outside. Eventually the matron came and sat beside me. Later in the afternoon Dad left and as I watched him disappear from view my heart sank but holding my head up high I was determined not to show it. Later that night when I was in bed, under the bedclothes I very quietly sobbed my little heart out.

Much later in life when Dad and I talked about these times and my adventurous escape, I reminded him that on our return to school he had spent a long time with the Headmaster. I asked him how the Head had responded to it all and what he'd said.

Dad replied, "He said if Woodhouse minor doesn't want Silcoates, then Silcoates doesn't want him."

Such arrogance.

I can assure him now that the feeling was mutual. Even from a boy who was only seven at the time.

Dad

Sunday Worship

Silcoates School was initially an independent boarding school for the sons of Ministers of The Congregational Church. It was an all-boys school and as such was very much male oriented. As I had spent most of my life with my sister as a close friend and companion I found living in such close proximity to all these males hard to adjust to. On Sunday morning I'd been used to walking down to the familiar Wicker Church in Sheffield with my dad. Now I found myself walking a long way, it seemed to me, with the whole school in regimental order to The Zion Congregational Church in Wakefield. When we arrived we all sat in a large group and endured the attentions of the congregation made up of mainly elderly ladies. The church was dark and usually cold in winter and I always found the addresses hard to comprehend. In later years when I heard the minister had been broadcasting the fact that his church was well attended, I thought "I'm not surprised when he had the whole of a school in residence every Sunday!"

There were no toilets available so you had to hope that you didn't require one or if you did, were able to get back to school before you wet your pants.

After Sunday lunch there was writing a letter to home time. We were required to pen some pleasant thoughts about the week that had passed and it was censored by the Housemaster in case anyone wrote 'Help!'

I wrote my letter in my form room and had to take it to my brother David so we could put both letters in the same envelope to save postage. It was good to see him but our meetings were always brief and talking strictly restricted. Most Sundays followed the same pattern.

A Bully in Sheep's Clothing

I realised soon enough that I had better try and make the best of my situation and I tried so hard to fit in to a regime that was so foreign to the love and joy I'd experienced so far in my life. I missed my sister and my mum and dad and the assurances that Gran gave me. Here it seemed I was going to be caught up in a sort of military order that was quite foreign to my lifestyle. We were ruled by bells. A clanging bell to get up, a bell for early morning prep, a bell to line up for breakfast, a bell for lessons and so on throughout the day. I began to integrate with the other boys of my own age and made a few special friends but I was always aware of the hierarchy that seemed to exist and that I should beware of boys who were monitors and especially the prefects. The prefects seemed to be a race apart and had unprecedented power. They seemed to consider that they had the right to beat small unhappy boys like myself and they did whenever you stepped out of line. I remember one incident that was etched on my mind for years afterwards.

When the bell rang for bed for the junior children, we had to line up at the bottom of the stair well and being instructed by a senior we made our way to our dormitory. We put on our pyjamas and went directly to the wash basins to brush our teeth and have a wash before bed. Each boy was inspected by a monitor or prefect to make sure he had done a thorough job. Not everyone passed this inspection, but eventually on this night we made it to the dormitory without incident.

I was soon in bed and nearly asleep when there was a great banging and a loud voice shouted "Right, all out, and line up, line up here in front of Watson's bed!"

What for, I wondered.

"I'll teach you lot for talking after Knock Up!"

Apparently, it was considered a crime to talk after there had been a knock on the dormitory door and this prefect and I'll always remember his name, Oddie major, had been listening for voices.

I wasn't sure why we had to line up in front of Watson's bed, but it soon became clear.

Oddie stood there with a shoe in his hand and he had brought in his buddie to hold us all over Watson's bed. He beat our backsides unmercifully as his buddy held us and looked on. In those days we seemed to have no redress. Such was the bullying culture of Silcoates.

Every night Matron looked at our bottoms, when we had a bath, and asked "Why have you all got such horrific bruises?" and she cast a tear when she knew.

Cross Country Run

There were two so-called houses in school Moores and Youngs and I was allocated to be in Youngs, probably because my brother was in Youngs as well. There was quite a lot of competitive spirit between the houses and throughout the term points could be acquired for your house for all kinds of outstanding individual achievements. These were added up at the end of each term and the house with the highest points was awarded the house shield. Sports Day and the days leading up to it were a living nightmare for me as I seemed to be absolutely hopeless at all manner of activities which could score points for your house. There were set attainment levels for long jump, hundred yards sprinting, discus throwing and all sorts of sporty activities. Points fell at the feet in great numbers for the athletes among us, usually accompanied by encouraging words.

"O well done, Hardcastle minor." Or whatever name it was.

"Woodhouse minor, have you not gained any points?"

"Sorry Sir, not yet,"

"Surely you can do better, try harder man, think of the house!"

I did think of the house and was reminded all the time of my lack of points and I was beginning to feel persecuted because of my inability at any kind of sport. It kept me awake at night and was on my every waking thought. "No points, no points!"

One day I was talking to a friend who like myself was not good at sport and we decided upon a careful but dishonest plan to try and get at least one point to let us off the hook. It was a deceitful move but looking back over the years I consider that we were driven to it and we hoped it would stop the persecution we were suffering.

The school had a free afternoon every Wednesday. This was because we had lessons on Saturday mornings.

Neither of us were any good at cross country running but we figured that if we ran about a third of the way around the course and hid for a little while in the bushes, then we could set off back at a steady pace and return within the allotted time, thus gaining a point for the house. So on a Wednesday afternoon the Housemaster set us off and wished us good luck.

Soon we were pretty tired but reached our objective at the top of the hill in the bushes. After sitting for a while we began to regret our misdeed and decided it wasn't a good idea as we considered the shame of us being found out. If we set off now, we would surely be too late back to pick up a point and so all would be well.

"Alright," we said, "let's go and take it easy on the way back."

"Hey, what are you two doing? Where ya runnin' to?"

Oh, no. Just our rotten luck. Running down the hill to catch up with us was the groundsman's son who was a keen runner himself and was in the local running club, the Greyhounds.

"What you doin?"

"We thought we would try to get a point for the house by running round our cross country," I called.

"Well come on," he said, "I'll help ya."

"No," I said, "I'm shattered."

"Come on," he shouted and he started to push both of us forward.

I lingered back as I just didn't want to go through with this but on we went and eventually my friend reached the school gates and the Housemaster said, "Well done you've just made it. Sorry Woodhouse minor you are just out and didn't make it."

I wasn't sorry at all and felt as though I had regained my honesty. Unfortunately, he caught up with me later in the evening and said that he thought his watch was fast and I had made it after all.

My friend and I kept mum and this is the first time it's ever been mentioned. I still feel slightly guilty.

Solo Performance

I did have some happy days that encouraged my love of music. We were very fortunate to have a first class Music Master at the time. He seemed a very kindly gentleman with quite a tubby build and a face that always looked content and he demonstrated his musical genius in many ways, not least in directing the school choir.

One day I plucked up the courage to ask him if there was any chance that I may audition for the choir. His affirmative answer lead me forth on a lifetime's adventure in music participation and appreciation. He became a lifelong friend and in later life an honoured guest at my wedding. My only regret is that he suffered a fatal heart attack and didn't live long enough to see my children.

After that initial audition for the school choir he told me that I had a supreme singing voice, in fact it was outstanding and he offered to give me singing lessons. I was beside myself. He took me under his wing and developed my singing to a professional level. After the first song I learned which was "Drink to me only with thine eyes" we went on to learn the classics and several anthems for which I always took the solo lead in the chapel on Sundays. These anthems I can sing even now "Come holy Ghost," and "Turn thy face from thy sins", I always looked over at Oddie major when I sang that one. I may not have been very good at football and games, I disliked them intensely, but when I sang my heart soared and I was lifted above into realms beyond and way above all the unhappiness I often felt.

I think at the time my singing gave me something to contribute to school life. I spent some considerable time learning the aria of "The Trout" by Shubert and eventually Dr Saunders told me that I'd be performing this at the school's Speech Day. What an honour, I was really looking forward to this. On the day the school hall was full and I even had my name in the programme. When my performance was announced I stood with arms by my side as I had been trained and sang. I sang like never before and the applause was rapturous. I looked across to my friend Dr Saunders and in my heart I thanked him, my dear friend, for all his encouragement and support that had made this moment.

Afterwards Dad said he had taken a photo of me singing, but it turned out a bit out of focus.

My sister who had been there said, "I'm really proud of you Andrew."

That was enough for me.

I loved music and painting and found great comfort in these activities. They were becoming part of my life and brought me much joy. No one could find fault with the gift I'd been given to sing with such grace and clarity and this was greatly encouraged. I took all the solos in the school choir and my friend Dr Saunders took me to many of his concerts outside school hours to give me an insight into professional choral work. One performance of "Haydn's Creation" by the Huddersfield Choral Society will always remain in my memory, especially the chorus of "The heavens are telling the glory of God."

He was a kind man and made a real impression on me amidst all the disruptions that seemed to be assaulting my soul at this time. I don't think looking back that Silcoates offered anything to me but a great big disruption to my developing mind.

Only one great soul, Dr Saunders, showed any normal compassion to me and to him now be the glory. My life at this time embraced the new and unfamiliar sound of music. It was fantasy and reality combined and every time I went for my singing time at Silcoates with my friend Dr Saunders my soul too found new possibilities and I was thankful to God for this developing friendship.

My singing voice was declared very special by most of the Masters at Silcoates. I didn't know it at the time but the boarders said kind things about it too. I do remember an incident when I sang very badly in chapel. It was the opening of the anthem "Come Holy Ghost". Dr Saunders said that he had had a lot of comments. I said perhaps it was probably that I had shouted too much at the recent football match.

"However much you feel enthusiastic, try not to do that again. Your voice is precious."

The out of focus photo of Andrew singing "the Trout", Silcoates Speech day 1949

Dreaded Dentist

Wednesday was a half day of studies leaving the afternoon free for pursuing personal interests and activities. Sometimes you were allowed into town to see a film at the cinema if you had enough pocket money to afford it. I remember my friend and myself asking the Housemaster if we could go to watch "Little Women" at the Plaza in Westgate.

"Little Women, Woodhouse? What sort of film is that?"

After I'd explained it was from the novel by Louisa May Alcott set in post-civil war America he went off to check this in the staff room and came back to us with permission. For weeks afterwards I was saddened by the death of Beth in the film and fell in love with Margaret O'Brien. For many of us Wednesday afternoons were times of escape from the confines of school life, though many sporting characters used this time to further their skills.

All these opportunities offered a kind of relief but what kept my own happiness at bay was my sense of undeserved pleasure instilled in me by the critical and almost distaining attitude of the place in which I found myself. These afternoon times had jeopardy as well. To lose the afternoon of freedom was a punishment to be avoided. It was the ultimate sanction but freely used by senior prefects and staff and some kind of work had to be undertaken. But fear arrived in the early afternoon, and if you were unlucky enough you had to sit in a classroom and wait for fear to arrive and so it did. At two o'clock uneven footsteps could be heard limping along the marble floor of the corridor dragging some sort of apparatus. The footsteps belonged to an old man who was short in stature and stooped low. He had white hair and a very pale face with a prominent nose and he was pulling his apparatus behind him. In many ways he was the image of Quilp in Dickens "The Old Curiosity Shop" who described him as being "...stubble-chinned, misshapen and cruel".

All of us were frightened by his appearance as he staggered into the classroom of the waiting boys. This was fear and this was the dentist!

Unfortunately, we all had to sit in this room and watch our friends being tortured. By the time it was my turn I just shut my eyes and hoped for the best. If a filling was needed, God help you. The apparatus he dragged behind him was a portable drill and he used to operate it using a treadle with his foot. But he couldn't keep it going because his foot got tired and so it slowed the drill action and often stopped altogether, prolonging the agony.

"Get a haircut Woodhouse minor", was another fear I dreaded. The hairdresser also took up our time on Wednesday afternoons. Again we had to sit and wait in a classroom for him to arrive. No apparatus was needed, only a pair of scissors and a couple of blunt hand held clippers.

"Right," he said, "let's have you one at a time gentleman," and the cries began that lasted all afternoon until the last boy had been shorn.

I think he probably got cramp in his clipper hand as he kept stopping for a rest and seemed to be pulling at your hair rather than cutting it. It was remarkable how he managed to give all of us the same haircuts. Very short back and sides.

Gardening Desires

I began to think my talents lay elsewhere and as there seemed to be some interest amongst the boarders in gardening I thought I'd apply for a plot to grow a few flowers. I was encouraged by the groundsman Mr Gouche and I was given a strip of garden along the main entrance of the school. It was in a dip outside the Headmaster's house and already had a few plants in it. My friend Willy Watson said he would like to share it with me and so we kept it very neat and tidy and weed free. In fact, we spent much of our time weeding rather than growing, although Mr Gouche gave us the odd plant.

Going down to the garden was a short soil path and then another soil path along the bottom of it. Both Willy and I thought this would be much more attractive if it was grassed over. So one Saturday afternoon in our free time we borrowed a spade and a wheelbarrow from Mr Gouche and wheeled it down the road to a grassy field. Here we cut out some good sized sods of grass and took them back to the garden. It took several trips until we had enough for the path and it looked really splendid.

Returning the spade and wheelbarrow we went back to have a further look and several of our friends had stopped to admire our handy work. Then we went in for tea.

"Woodhouse! Watson!" A voice rang out.

"Woodhouse! Watson! Come out here."

Lord, it was Odd Dick, head of lower school. Odd Dick was the nickname he had acquired. Nobody knew why except his real name was Richard Richardson and he was thought to be an "odd bod" by most of the boys. His reputation wasn't helped by the rumour that one night in an inebriated state he had stood at the bottom of the stairs leading to the dormitories shouting for a lift.

He had a bit of an aggressive side as well and it was he who had given Oddie major, the prefect, the go ahead to tan us all for talking after "knock up".

We were marched to our little garden and he pointed at the grass turfs. "Where did you get these?"

"Please sir, we brought them here from the field down the road this afternoon. We thought they made the garden more attractive."

"And what do we say to the farmer when he finds half the grass in his field gone?"

Wow, I didn't think we had taken that much.

"Well, Watson and Woodhouse minor what are you going to say to him?"

"We'll say sorry sir."

"Exactly!"

His face was getting redder. A bad sign. "Well you can go and get the barrow and spade and put it all back now! Go on and be quick!"

As we scuttled off he shouted, "I'm surprised at you Watson, I thought you had more sense."

Presumably he took it for granted that I had none. It took us ages to return the grass sods to the field and eventually get some sleep. Nothing more was mentioned about the incident but I kept my distance from Odd Dick for some time after that. Sometimes when things go wrong in my life I allow myself to mutter "Oh sod it!". It has historical roots!

Rigged Competition

As a boarder at Silcoates I remember well a painting I became engrossed in following my entry into a painting competition. I loved painting and creating objective and imaginative images of recollected scenes. I painted the market at Pontefract from memory and I thought this was a winner. It really was outstanding and considering my future as a professional artist displayed much talent.

"Your work is quite outstanding Woodhouse minor, but I cannot say you are a winner of this competition, because where you should have painted white you have used the white of the paper.

"But Sir there was no white paint available!"

The next competition required the making of a model aeroplane. I consulted my brother David and some of his friends about this and all of them offered to help. Cardboard, glue and inks, paper clips and all sorts were offered to me for this great project. We worked for hours and hours and we made a fantastic plane beautifully coloured and displayed so well on the competition stand.

"Well done, every boy for these magnificent efforts. You are all worthy winners, but the prize goes to Hardcastle minor. The worthiest winner.

"But sir, he bought his plane from a shop!"

Keeping to the Rules

Looking back on those days as a boarder I wonder sometimes how we all survived the experience. I think the whole idea was to "make a man of you," but I think now some of the methods were out of order and definitely very unpleasant. In the whole of my time there I found there was nowhere available to chill out or relax.

Dormitories were out of bounds during daylight hours and there was no common room for students. The only place to sit was the form room or the field and the latter was impossible in winter.

The bell to wake up in the morning was sounded at seven o'clock and everyone rose like clockwork. If, however, you had been apprehended for a previous misdemeanour then a favourite punishment given out by staff and prefects alike was to take an early run around the periphery of the school boundaries in PE kit. This had to be achieved before the rising bell and in all weathers. It was not very pleasant for a young boy to run this course alone sometimes in the early darkness of winter. Even worse was that in those days there were no showers in the bathrooms and certainly no bath was allowed, so it was uncomfortable for the rest of the day.

Not all days were fraught I did have some jollity although it always seemed to be short lived. The school encouraged participation in sport and I did my best to join in despite the fact that I seemed to be uncoordinated and clumsy. I came to accept the fact that I was always chosen last, by default, to be on one side or the other in team games, especially football. I quite enjoyed rugby because it seemed to have more purpose and variety than football and I was small enough to make a good hooker. I used to say "it's fun in the scrum" and it seemed to me it was a more exciting game than football. I was hopeless at throwing myself on the ground to make a good tackle but some of the other boys were brilliant at this. I was always frightened that I might hit my face on the ground or even break a leg. My body just wouldn't respond to such rash acts and as much as I wanted to I was scared to have a go. In any case I couldn't see the benefit of kicking a bladder full of air around a field for hours at a time.

Cricket was the sport in the summer months and I faired reasonably well as a batsman. When I took up a bat and was on the crease I always went through the ritual of asking for centre for my bat. I held it there in front of the stumps while the umpire called out left a bit, right a bit, until finally he said "right, that's central."

I always smiled to myself because it made no difference to my performance. I only did this for effect and if I hit the ball I considered myself lucky. If I hit the ball and managed a couple of runs and my team mates called out "Oh well done Woodhouse" I felt I belonged to the inner circle.

One cricket match I was in will always be a source of happy memories to me. I hadn't been very involved and my batting was appalling, I think I was out for a duck. It was a very hot day and I was about to fall asleep on my feet when a voice shattered my somnolence.

" Woodhouse, are you asleep, or are you fielding? Wake up man." It was Mr Chadwick.

"O dear," I thought, "here we go again."

"Woodhouse, take a turn bowling."

I didn't want to with Mr Chadwick watching and my team knowing how hopeless I was. But I said, "Yes Sir" and I heard a few moans from my team mates.

I waited for the end of the over and someone threw me the ball. I ran about a mile before I delivered the ball and it shot up into the air about six feet right of the stumps.

"Wide!"

My next ball shot up into the air about six feet left of the stumps.

"Wide!"

The next ball narrowly missed Mr Chadwick.

"Wait, Woodhouse wait, before you kill us all!"

"Forget the over arm bowling. Just try some under arm bowling and try to get your eye in. No need to run half a mile to deliver these, just stand up to the crease and for heaven's sake, bowl gently!"

I did as I was advised and sent one or two balls down the pitch that were remarkably near the stumps. Soon I was beginning to enjoy the game. At least I thought I was getting the hang of it and although the opposing batsmen were scoring runs off me I was reasonably accurate in my aim. My first over completed I returned to fielding with one or two calls of "well tried Woodie. You were much better at under arm. Well done!"

But I wasn't finished yet. I was given another over and off I went again bowling under arm. This time I had a method. I had become quite accurate and instead of trying to bounce the ball onto the stumps I tried to let it bounce first and then gently glide along the grass into the stumps. This was a deadly procedure because it was almost impossible to stop the ball with the bat and it gently rolled up to the stumps, much to the annoyance of the batsman.

"Out!" was called at least four times in that over and appeals to Mr Chadwick were of no avail.

"But Sir, Woodhouse is sending down grass cutters and we can't hit the ball at all!"

"So?" replied Mr Chadwick, "He's not breaking the rules, just carry on and let someone else bowl now".

And they did, but not before I noticed the smile on Mr Chadwick's face when he looked across at me.

Ready, Steady, Go

When I was head of my first Primary School I was determined to make Sports Day fun for everyone whatever the child's ability. Those who were good shone and those who were as hopeless as I had been in my childhood got lots of encouragement and support.

My first Primary School had about one hundred and twenty children so it was fairly small in size. The staff were eager to make our Sports Day a happy occasion and soon rallied round to the cause. It became something we all began to look forward to and become enthusiastic about. In the past it hadn't ranked highly as an event but now it did. Flags were made and refreshments considered and after a kindly word in our groundsman's ear he agreed to line out tracks around the field.

We had to have a rehearsal with the children a few days before Sports Day because lining up in tracks and knowing where to be on the day was all new to them. With the help of staff and the older children I managed to sort out the whole of the school on the field with the infants right at the front in separate lines within their tracks.

By this time, I had a megaphone and I told them, "Listen carefully, very carefully. When I say ready steady go, I want the front line only to run as fast as you can to your teacher Mrs Jackson who is standing over there at the top of the field. Just the children on the front line. Can you see her?"

"Yes, Mr Woodhouse," they all replied in a deafening chorus, "Yes!"

"Right, then," I said, "let's try it."

"Ready, steady, GO!"

And with that the WHOLE school raced up the field.

It was some time before I lived that down, it was a good tale to tell at my expense. But it was fun and come the Sports Day all the Mums and Dads said it had been a great afternoon and a lovely atmosphere. Even the Dad's race was a great success.

Did I enter that? I thought not. Best to give someone else a chance!

Autumn Wood

Bluebell Wood

Garden Border

Path Through Bluebell Wood

The Allotments

Walk Through Woods

Winter Wonderland

Winter

School Sports

Ihad three headships in my career in Primary Education. The third headship was of a large school and in the past sport, especially football, ranked very highly on the agenda. The school had a tradition of sporting activities and I'd taken over from a head who seemed to live for football. I'd been at this school in the past as an assistant, responsible for team leadership and music, including the establishment of a choir. Sport was not on my immediate timetable then, but now here I was responding to the requests to make our Sports Day memorable. At the time I had a very enthusiastic Deputy Head and between us we came up with what we thought was a jolly good idea. There would of course be all the familiar apparatus and usual race tracks and seats were to be set up for parents along the side of the track so they could all have a good view of all the events. A few special chairs would be set up at the top of the field for any visiting governors. Our plan was to open the games with something special. So we organised loud speakers to broadcast the music from "The loneliness of the long distance runner" and I arranged for some fireworks and rockets to open the games.

On the afternoon of the day there was a good deal of excitement amongst the children. Someone must have found out about my rockets because word had got around. When the games were about to begin we switched on the ghetto blaster and a great sound filled the field.

The children cheered and clapped knowing the games were at last about to begin, but not before my firework display. First a few Catherine Wheels and one or two volcanoes and cascades and then my finale. The first two rockets rose into the sky on their way to Mars amid more cheers! I felt my children really appreciated my efforts. The last rocket was lit and off it went.

A silence fell over the field, an eerie hush. In horror I watched as the rocket, far from rising into the air, shot across the field at about five feet from the ground and made its alarming course directly to the Governors seats. A gasp went up from the spectators around the field as it shot up suddenly into the air and exploded above the head of Mrs Peabody, an elderly and respected governor.

Unfortunately, all the children gave the biggest cheer of the afternoon, and I had to dash across to make my peace with this dear governor.

Thankfully, she saw the funny side of it all and said that was the first time in her life she had been fired upon!

The rest of the afternoon passed without incident, and I decided that on future Sports Days I should just welcome everybody and then start the first race.

Good News

It was holiday time again and I woke up in a really comfy bed looking out at a beautiful sky through our bedroom window. I shared the tiny room with my sister Margaret. I just happened to have a window in front of my bed and dear Margaret looked at the door, because her bed faced the other way.

She asked me that morning why I was looking so happy and I said that I didn't know. I just felt that something wonderful was about to happen today. To make things even more wonderful I said that I was sure that I had seen a face up there in the clouds of the morning and that face looked like the face of Jesus.

"Wow, Andrew," I can't believe what you've just said, "you are so strange, sometimes."

Later in the morning Margaret persuaded me to go for a walk with her. I wasn't keen to walk anywhere but I went and we strolled through the grounds of Pontefract Castle.

There's nothing better than a loving sister who is a dear friend as well. This day I felt very much at peace. The sun was warm, the flowers gave out their scents and heaven was about us.

Margaret seemed to be on the edge of saying something that was on her mind. She stopped walking and put her arm around me. I wondered why. Then as the sun suddenly burst across my face and I could see nothing but a dazzling light she held back no longer.

She said in a soft voice that was so characteristic of her, "Andrew listen to me. I'm not supposed to say anything at the moment, but it may be that you'll have to leave Silcoates as Dad can't afford to pay for you anymore. David is going to Kelham to train for the ministry and so you would be on your own you wouldn't like that would you? Dad thinks you may be better living at home. Don't say anything when we get back will you? Pretend I haven't said anything."

"Wow," I thought. "That's the best bit of news I've heard in the past few years."

Dreaded Eleven Plus

I returned to school that term with a light heart. My Dad had seemed a bit concerned for my future, but not me. I'd found out last holiday that my brother David was to leave this term too as he'd been accepted into The Theological College of Kelham to begin training for the Anglican ministry.

Both of us it seemed would be leaving at the end of term. I had one last task to perform, just one more hoop to jump through. Upon leaving Silcoates Dad expected me to gain entrance to a Grammar school and the most convenient was in Pontefract itself, King's School. I could walk quite easily from where we lived so that was to be my immediate destiny.

I was surprised that I was beginning to have mixed feelings about leaving Silcoates. In spite of everything I began to feel that maybe I may miss this place after all, but the feelings didn't last.

"Woodhouse, I understand you're to sit the eleven plus exam for entry into Grammar school. I've been asked to give you some extra tuition to help you."

Mr Whitwam took me into my form room one Saturday afternoon and really did his best to explain all about the eleven plus. He set me all sorts of puzzles and mathematical problems that I'd face in the test, but I just couldn't understand the format of the questions or the point of it all. My mind became so blurred and vacant that in the end he gave up his task and wished me good luck anyway, in the manner of a failed General sending an unequipped man out to overcome unbeatable foes.

And so on the day of the exam I was taken by one of the Masters to the local Primary School. I was wearing my school uniform which seemed to cause a bit of interest amongst the children already sitting on chairs looking very ready indeed to face anything this eleven plus may throw at them.

I felt nervous as the Master from Silcoates left and I was on my own. I was now forced to be with other children, who were labelled for some reason as Potskids by my so-called elite friends back at school. I was now one of them and I was very uncomfortable because we weren't encouraged to mix with any other children outside of our closed school environment.

I said hello to the group and noticed some of the girls and most of the boys were having a silent giggle at me. All I could think about was home. I wanted my Mum.

It was over and I managed to put my hands over my answers and my writing to try to keep it secret from prying eyes. As for myself, I think at this point I was praying!

There was a very sympathetic teacher who gathered in the papers and asked me to fill in my address on the exam paper. I hadn't seen that I had to do this before because I'd been so nervous. When I'd filled this in he looked at the address I'd written and asked me if anyone had ever shown me how to spell the place where I lived. I had put The Mance instead of Manse and this caused a few tuts from my new acquaintances. I remembered how to spell it from that day on.

Putting his hand on my shoulder the teacher said, "Never mind Andrew, I think this has all been a bit of a strange experience for you." This made me feel much better.

I think that I would've liked to have got to know my new acquaintances better but as soon as the exam was over they disappeared and I was on my own. I found a chair to sit on and the teacher sorted some papers at his desk. As I sat there I pondered on my future especially if I was to fail this test and inside I felt that I hadn't done all that well.

The end of term arrived. I said my goodbyes and I made a special effort to thank my friend Dr Saunders for all he'd done for me. School gathered in the Hall for a short talk by the Headmaster and he wished all the leavers, including myself, success in our future lives.

We joined arms and sang Auld Lang Syne, had three cheers for school and then made our way out into the new world that awaited us. At last I was homeward bound and hopefully for good.

A Kind Headmaster

"Bit of bad news Andrew," said Dad, "You didn't pass the eleven plus."

I had a feeling I wouldn't pass so it came as no surprise. But what was I to do now? Dad was really upset about it and I often heard Mum and Dad locked in serious discussion about my future. Kings School was now out of the question and they didn't want me to go to a Secondary School for some reason and so it seemed to me that I was a bit in limbo. But, I wasn't to be in limbo for long.

I was mooching around at home one afternoon wondering what to do when Dad appeared.

"Good news," he said, "I've got some really good news. I've just come from a meeting with the Headmaster of Queen Elizabeth's Grammar School in Wakefield and he's agreed to take you in as a pupil. He's such a kind man. But he'd like to meet you and I've arranged for you to go over with me next Wednesday."

"Have you really been all that way today Dad? To Wakefield on the bus?"

"Yes I have. So next Wednesday, you'll be on your best behaviour and be very polite, won't you, Andrew?"

"Of course Dad and thank you so much. Wakefield Grammar, wow!"

I had to admire Dad for taking all that trouble for me and I felt that I mustn't let him down.

That Wednesday we caught the bus into Wakefield. It felt strange to be back in the same city as Silcoates and heading for a school that used to be a rival on the sports field.

As we entered the school gates I was impressed by the building itself that looked slightly Elizabethan in style. The drive ended at the entrance door and as we ascended the steps we were met by a lady who welcomed us and took us into the office.

"Mr Grace won't be long," she said, "and he's looking forward to meeting you."

I warmed to this lady very much and I felt so at ease in the presence of Mr Grace. He spoke quite softly and smiled at me several times as I answered his questions.

After sometime he said, "Welcome to our school Andrew. I hope you settle down quickly and enjoy being with us."

It was a refreshing change to be called Andrew instead of Woodhouse minor and I was beginning to feel at home already.

Dad shook Mr Grace's hand and said his farewells and also expressed his gratitude to the headmaster for taking me in. We said goodbye to the ladies in the office as well and strode out of the gates into the city of Wakefield with happy hearts.

"Thank God, thank God," Dad kept saying and so I echoed the same sentiments, "Thank God, thank God," as we almost skipped down the street.

We eventually reached home and we had to recount our meeting blow by blow to Mum and Gran. My sister Margaret was pleased as well. But there was no one more pleased than I. Mum said that I'd have to get up early to catch the bus to Wakefield every day.

"Don't forget you have to be there on a Saturday morning as well."

"That's nothing," I thought. "At least I'll be able to come back here afterwards. Back here. Back home."

"There's just one more thing to be done," Dad said, "because you didn't pass the eleven plus you have to have an intelligence test to see how clever you are. They want to test your IQ but you'll be alright Andrew. So I have to arrange an appointment with a psychologist."

"A what?"

"A psychologist."

"What's he going to do and what's an IQ?"

"All he's going to do is take a measure of your behaviour and your mental abilities by giving you some short tests. You'll be fine. Don't worry."

Dad

Mr Bone

The day of my visit to the psychologist arrived and I was told to put my best school uniform on. Mum inspected me and declared that I looked very respectable, "our Andrew" she always called me our Andrew when she wanted me to know that she was proud of me. I don't think that dressing up in my best would necessarily increase my intelligence but at least I felt presentable. I left home with my Dad and I was feeling confident. In some ways I was looking forward to proving my worth.

"Bye Mum and Gran," I called over my shoulder, and

"Bye Margaret, see you back home again for tea!"

So Dad and I set forth.

We caught the bus to Wakefield and walked along several streets until we arrived at our destination.

There was a brass plaque that had names engraved on it set in the red bricked wall beside a large black door. Dad rang the doorbell several times and eventually the door was opened by a small untidily dressed gentleman in a black suit, carrying a bunch of papers in his hand. He reminded me of Smike in Nicholas Nickleby.

"Yes," he said "can I help?"

Dad told him that we'd come to see Mr Bone the psychologist, to which he replied "Ah, yes. What name is it?"

"Woodhouse," said Dad, "Andrew Woodhouse."

"Yeees," he emphasized the word, "yeees, I will go and let Mr Bone know you have arrived."

At that he shuffled up a very old and dusty staircase that looked as though it was from a scene in a Dickens movie. I noticed that the windows were really dirty and also the bench we were invited to sit upon was well worn and ancient.

"Hello, hello, hello," a voice called out from above stairs, "do come on up, and mind the uneven steps."

I was not impressed at all and even less sure when this last clarion call was followed by a strange subdued hysterical laughter. I looked at Dad and he just shrugged his shoulders and together we ascended the stairs.

Mr Bone was a tall man. He wore a brown suit, worse for wear and I noticed that he had leather patches sewn to the elbows. Why had I made the effort to look so clean and presentable in my Sunday best?

His office was full of boxes and papers. They were all over the place. Every space appeared to be full of paper. Dad and I were eventually found a chair to sit on and Mr Bone began his task.

"Welcome, Andrew, to my world of psychology!"

I looked at Dad who was beginning to look as apprehensive as me.

"Andrew, I really want to get the best from you and so I hope you can relax."

I was very relaxed as he made his first moves.

I don't know to this day what he was on about. I didn't understand his questions or what he expected of me. I considered him to be in a world of his own. I felt my world was more rooted in reality than his.

I noticed his tuts and moans were increasing and his pencil started to record less and less of my answers to the problems I was supposed to be solving. I just didn't understand why we had to solve make believe problems in the first place.

Eventually we had a slight disagreement. One of the questions he asked me was totally incomprehensible.

"Andrew, a boy called William who lived at the top of a hill walked down twenty yards to the river and filled his bucket that held two gallons of water. He then returned to the top of the hill carrying the water, but his bucket had two holes in it and on the way back up the hill he lost two pints every two yards. How much water had he in his bucket by the time he reached the top of the hill?

I eventually said to him.

"That's a silly story, Mr Bone, anyone who has any intelligence at all wouldn't use a bucket with a hole in it to carry water and this one had two holes in it."

After that the testing came to an end and Dad thanked him. Mr Bone said he would let Dad know the results and his assessment of the tests and he would forward a copy to my new school. He rang a small hand bell and "Smike" entered the room and guided us out of the building.

Many years later my Dad said to me he'd had a note from Mr Bone to say that I hadn't got enough intelligence to get me across the road!

Dad's Idea of a Great Holiday

It was the beginning of the school holiday and so I'd have to wait until September before starting Queen Elizabeth's at Wakefield. But I was in no hurry. In any case there was lots to explore in Pontefract.

There seemed to be a lot of interesting places including the castle where Richard the Second was supposed to have been murdered. There was a racecourse that sounded attractive but more than anything there was a large park with a large lake with boats for hire. That sounded great as I fancied taking a boat out.

Gran had already taken my sister and me to the market in town.

"Tell you what," she said. "do you fancy some Liquorice Allsorts and some Pontefract cakes?"

"What are those?" I asked, "Are they like buns?"

"Ee, no," she said, "they're made of liquorice. Pontefract is famous for sweets made from liquorice. Didn't you know?"

"No I didn't, but come to think of it, I remember reading a poem by John Betjeman called 'The Liquorice Fields of Pontefract'."

Every summer time we always went away on holiday.

"This year," Dad said, "we're going to Silverdale for a fortnight. We've arranged to stay in a Bed and Breakfast owned by two very nice ladies. Mrs and Miss Kay, mother and daughter. They live in a lovely big house just outside of Silverdale but it's some way from the beach."

There were six of us altogether in our family at this time and preparations for a family holiday took some organising. My mother had this strange notion that for at least two weeks before departure we had to wear our oldest clothes in order to give her time to make sure that the clothes scheduled to be worn on holiday were clean and ready for packing.

I'd already made one or two friends in town and passing them in the street or even stopping for a chat they all recognised the pattern of wearing old clothes before a holiday.

"Going on holiday Andrew?"

"Yes, how can you tell?"

"Don't worry, my Mum's the same. Holidays mean old clothes before, clean clothes on holiday."

I found this a very odd practice and one many families followed. But who was I to complain, I was very happy to be home.

There was a sort of heightened expectation as the time for our holiday drew near. Mum and Gran seemed to have turned into a laundry machine and walked around ticking off lists. Dad seemed engrossed in paper work and my sister Margaret and I enjoyed the time as Mum and Dad seemed very happy.

My brother David, I thought, was a bit aloof, saying little and taking all this excitement in his stride. As he was about to embark on training for ministry he spent a considerable time with our local vicar. But it was good to be together and in later life I realised that it was a magical time. When I had a family of my own, I was advised by so many of my friends and family that it was important to have a holiday together. Such good advice. But I already knew how essential it was. Holidays I found, strengthened love.

"Cases Hector? Have you got the cases down?"

"They're all under the stairs. Do you want them now?"

"I do, come on."

It's beginning to be serious when cases are called for, "Time draweth near!"

Out they all came, mainly brown leather and well worn.

"We'll need at least six," said Mum "and there's only five. "I tell you what, why don't we take our Andrew's trunk he had at boarding school? We'd get a lot of clothes in that."

"What? You don't really mean that do you. Who's going to carry it? Gran?"

Gran looked disgusted with the silly suggestion. But we all fell about laughing at Mum's silly proposition. But I don't think she really meant it. I knew she was joking.

The night before our departure I didn't get any sleep. I don't think many of us had much sleep because we were very excited and really looking forward to this holiday.

"Wow, that was a short night. I hardly slept a wink, is it really morning?"

Suddenly I was aware of noisy crashing about and voices raised in expectation.

"How long are you going to be in that bathroom?"

"Who's taken my hair brush?"

"I can't find the key to this case!"

"Make sure Gran has her pills!"

So many requests and exclamations that it sounded like a voice orchestra singing deliberately loud and out of tune. I pushed my bedroom door shut and put my head back on the pillow and thought I had escaped the turmoil, but no.

"Andrew, are you up yet? If you don't get up, we'll leave you behind!"

I thought that I'd better show willing and so I made my way to the bathroom, but someone was in it.

"Are you going to be long, because I'm in danger of being left behind."

"What a good idea," called a voice that I instantly recognised as belonging to David. "Maybe we will leave you behind. Ha, Ha, Ha."

"That's not funny, hurry up."

After what seemed to be an age the door opened and I rushed inside. After a few splashes of water around my face I was soon out, dressed in my holiday clothes and ready for breakfast. Dad was chief chef today and he'd made a good breakfast for us all of bacon and eggs.

"You need a good breakfast when there's travelling to be done," he said and I agreed with him wholeheartedly.

There were times in our house when everybody seemed to be in a jolly mood and holiday time was one of them. Getting ready for departure intensified the urgency of getting everything right, so that nothing was overlooked and all that we may need on our adventures was carefully packed.

"Let's check everything before we leave."

"I've done all that."

"Right then, all hands to clearing up the breakfast things and we'll be off."

There was a great rush to clear the table, I've never seen it cleared so fast and all the pots and pans were soon washed and dried. Gran shook the tablecloth outside of the back door, folded it and put it into the dresser.

"Make sure you lock that door again, mother." my mum called out to Gran, "We don't want any burglars whilst we're away."

We all had something to carry.

In an orderly fashion we bungled out of the house and waited for the taxi to arrive. Dad couldn't drive so it was quite a treat to have a ride in a car and we had to have a taxi because we had so many cases and bags and the railway station was a long way away, at the other end of town.

"I hope he's not late," Mum said, "we don't want to miss the train."

"That would be awful."

"Don't say that."

"Oh my that's horrid."

"He'll be here soon."

"Oh no," called Dad, "I think I've left my camera inside on the dining room table, I'll have to go and get it."

"Oh Dad, be quick, be quick!"

He dashed off and was soon back but without the camera.

"Where on earth can it be? I must have put it in one of the bags. Everyone have a quick look, just look in the small bags."

We couldn't find it. Dad looked puzzled.

"Too late now here comes the taxi."

"Blimey, how long are you going away for? A month?"

We only just managed to squash all the cases and bags into the taxi then pushed and tugged ourselves in. To dad's delight his camera fell on the floor of the taxi.

"There it is!" he said.

"Maybe we ought to have ordered a larger taxi, but we've managed to get in," Dad muttered.

"A larger taxi?" said the driver. "A larger taxi? A double decker bus more like!"

We came to a stop and fell out of the doors grasping our luggage and dragging it to the barrier. Dad paid the taxi fare and we were soon standing on the station platform eagerly awaiting the steam engine to arrive.

"Did the taxi cost much?" asked Mum.

"It was two and sixpence – half a crown."

"Cor that's a lot," I said, "that's half my holiday money."

Suddenly there was a massive ear-piercing whistle as the train came rolling down the track.

Dad started to sing "Get on board little children," but Mum told him to shush she knew what Dad was like when he got carried away and sometimes I think she thought he may well be literally carried away for some things he did.

She said, "Don't be daft, everyone's looking at us."

But there was only a handful of travellers about and most of them looked half asleep.

"Mind the doors please," shouted the station master, "careful as you go."

Fortunately, we found an empty carriage and we helped Gran up first. After that it was all for one and one for all, as we all jostled to sit next to a window.

In those days the carriages had individual compartments accessed by sliding doors off a side corridor. These compartments were very cosy and had large comfortable seats facing each other. Above the seats were luggage racks made of netting and there were lovely photographs on the walls. The windows slid up and down, opened by pulling on a wide leather strap.

"We must remember to change at Carnforth," Dad said.

As the train gathered speed it made a rhythm on the tracks, a definite beat that came up into our carriage, only changing when it went over some points or passed a junction.

Listening to these sounds made me begin to feel sleepy. I was content to sleep without a care, surrounded by a loving family.

At the beach

Faster Than Fast

"Carnforth! Carnforth!"

I was awoken with a start. There was a hive of activity in our carriage.

"All change. All change."

"Are you awake, our Andrew. We're here at Carnforth. We get off here. Help your Gran. David, you bring that bag there if you can. No Margaret, I'll bring that one, you catch hold of that little brown case up there. Come on everybody. Off we go again."

"Mind the gap as you step onto the station. Mind the gap," the porter called and we all managed to mind the gap and we heaved our heavy loads, cases and bags, along the platform to await our next connection that would take us to our real destination of Silverdale.

The next train arrived promptly and we dragged our cases and bags, onto and into another carriage, took our seats, secured our heavy bags and cases and cheered as the train pulled out of the station.

To this day I'm not sure why we cheered. But I suspect it was because we let gravity take over our luggage and we were for a brief time at least free from the burden.

"Won't be long now, about half an hour," said Dad.

"You're not going to sleep again are you Andrew," David said.

Now I was fully awake and aware I was more interested in the speed the train was travelling. It really was going very quickly and as I looked out of the window everything seemed to be blurred. Houses and trees and farms and woods flew by. It was hard to keep them in focus.

Eventually we arrived. Silverdale hadn't changed. The station was the same and the porter still called out "Welcome to Silverdale". The white railings needed a coat of paint, but the flowers in the station garden bloomed in their red display supported by an assortment of beautiful white daisies and pink roses. The porter's trolley was still there waiting for luggage. It was pushed and maneuvered with a rumbling characteristic of its worn and tired wheels by Frederick who had been in charge of it for many years. He pulled it towards us along the quiet and dusty platform.

He'd taken charge of this trolley as he considered it to be a part of his job, though it was widely known that it was his only job. He rolled it over to where we stood with our cases and bags in abundance, bags that still bulged in spite of the effort to flatten them a little.

"Do you want a taxi? If you do, you'll have to be quick 'cos Cedric's going off soon."

"Who's Cedric?"

"My brother."

Cedric soon had us on our way and delivered us to our destination. The welcome by our hosts was quite an amorous affair with much hugging and squeezing and enthusiastic words of friendship.

The Long Walk

We were woken early and after a jolly good breakfast a picnic was prepared with so much food packed I thought we must be getting ready to feed an army. There was eventually lots of bags full of food and drink including two enormous flasks. We then gathered in the hallway, collected our coats, in case it rained, and ladened down like a dromedary about to cross the Sahara, embarked on our pilgrimage for the day.

The sun was up and shining and our feet crunched the pebbled garden path as we made our way out of the gate onto the lane. This was a peaceful place and as we wandered along I really did feel that I'd captured the spirit of the earth and the embrace of the hedgerow and the wild flowers blooming beneath like chicks in a sheltering nest. Even the wild flowers growing along the stone walls that struggled for existence looked happy this morning.

It was already warm and the coats and bags we were wrestling with soon slowed us down on our pilgrimage. We were making for the edge of the marshes and we were pleased it wasn't too far to walk in the heat of the day. As we trundled around a corner of the lane, there came a high pitched female voice that startled us.

"I say, you look as though you are leaving home. You're not expecting rain as well are you?"

The voice came from a lady, who was engrossed in picking the fruit in her garden and her voice sounded very upper crust.

"You look terribly hot. I think you are staying at the Kay's, are you not? I'd simply love to show you my prize raspberries, they are enormous this year. Do come in through the wicket gate and I will fetch some cold juice for you all as well."

This seemed a grand opportunity for a short break and the prospect of adding interest to the day.

After all, there was no rush. The summer was with us and this was a lazy day with a sun that warmed to perfection.

Her garden greeted us with the sound of bees and frantic wasps and a dragonfly confident of protection in its borders. The scent of lavender was pungent by the kitchen window.

"I'm Mrs Vasey," she said, "yes, Mrs Vasey."

She seemed to have quite an affectionate manner with an air of being country bred. Her face looked tired but content and I wondered if she'd travelled a long way on her pilgrimage on this earth and having overcome all, was now happy to rest in her beloved garden.

She had a strange voice. It was very highly pitched and very plummy and David started taking off her voice but thankfully from a distance. Nevertheless, Margaret and I got the giggles and David did it even more.

I must say the drinks she provided were lovely and refreshing and we thanked her profusely. Her garden was full of all kinds of fruit and beautiful flowers and was such a wonderful experience. It was how I'd always imagined the Garden of Eden to be.

"When you pass here on your way home, do call in and I will let you have some of my prize raspberries for your tea."

And so we went on to the marshes. We still trundled along as we could do nothing else carrying our various loads. We went across the disciples' field, so called because there were twelve tall trees alongside the footpath and these were supposed to represent the disciples. David was still taking off the voice of Mrs Vasey talking about her raspberries which he did all afternoon. He was very good at achieving the perfect impersonation.

The tide was in at the marshes and so we found a lovely shaded spot to have our picnic. Mother always made sure it was well organised and Margaret was the chief giver outer of sandwiches. Gran had offered to buy us all an ice cream later on in the afternoon and when she made the announcement we all crooned, "Oooooooo!"

"Don't be daft," she said.

But she was enjoying herself.

Dad started to get out his camera.

"Here we go."

"How do you want us now Dad?"

"Well I tell you what children, get yourselves over there on that hill and I'll take a silly photo of you doing silly things."

It's a photo I treasure even today. Dad was good fun in his younger days and Mum the picnic specialist was so loving to us all.

That day we frolicked and it didn't matter if our clothes got muddy in the dykes or we managed to get green stains from the grass on our socks. It just didn't matter. We had such a great time. We even had a game of cricket and I was first in. My brother David never had an innings because he fell asleep on the grass.

Gran was true to her word and treated us all to the biggest ice creams in Silverdale and we had the raspberries for tea. Mum even bought cream to go with them. Good old Mum.

Dad being silly at Silverdale

Gran

Looking back on those childhood days Gran was a loving presence in our family. In fact, our family would not have been as rich without her. Although we didn't realise it at the time, she was a link with a bygone age and all the values of living that working class ladies had to endure in her generation. She was family orientated and was brought up to serve family life as an obedient wife, mother and Gran.

She told me tales of baking and selling bread from a wheelbarrow during the depression and taking in washing to try to keep her family from the breadline when her husband Ted died from diphtheria when he was only forty-two. As a young boy I found this very moving, but I was glad she was part of our family and lived with us.

In later years I admired Dad. It was his decision to invite her to be with him and Mum almost as soon as they were married. So she had been a part of our family as long as I could remember.

Gran was a bit of a character. She seemed to live a modest life. She was not a part of any group or organisation and didn't go to church very often. She seemed to enjoy preparing meals and making bread. It was considered to be very slovenly to buy bread in those days so most people made their own. She also made the Christmas puddings the old fashioned way by making sure there was a sixpence in each portion served. She was also in charge of making the mincemeat which smelt and tasted delicious and a great delight was giving it a stir and making a wish.

On Christmas Day we had to wait for Gran to get up to open her presents to us. Sometimes it was a long and impatient wait that seemed to go on for ages. We always knew what our presents were as we were given the same every year. They were snow houses. Large boxes covered in cotton wool and made to look like a dolls house covered in snow. Inside were a variety of games and toys and after the war there were some left over bits of equipment, such as goggles, a hat or a flag. Some would be banned today. I remember a wire gun made of a strong metal wire as used in modern coat hangers. You pushed a round pellet along the straight piece of wire until it was held in front of a powerful spring. Pull the trigger and it flew across the room at a pace! There was no protection at the end of the muzzle and it could easily have caused great damage to the user or anyone who happened to be in the way.

Gran often appeared to be detached from the general activities of the household. But she was very outspoken when she'd spent a long time cooking a meal and the guests hadn't turned up on time.

On answering the door she'd say, "We've 'ad ours."

They were often David's guests and he was mortified.

Sometimes when I wanted to go to watch a matinee with my friends and when I'd exhausted every source to obtain some money including Mum and Dad, Gran would often respond to my moaning. I pretended not to notice as she went upstairs to her bedroom and came down again with her hand in her apron pocket.

She'd squeeze a sixpence into my hand and say "Don't come again."

But I did and she knew I would. I began to think that she must have a stash of loot hidden in her room.

"You'll ruin that boy," Mum would say.

But Gran just winked at me.

Gran often made us laugh at some of her favourite sayings. She would say things like "By it's black over our Bill's mother's" and "By he's as lazy as Loveland's dog when it lays down to bark".

She didn't swear but when she got frustrated or felt the need to swear she would call out "O drot it, drot it."

Thunderstorms upset her and she used to go around the house covering up the mirrors because she said they attracted the lightning. When I was very small I used to try and find a room without a mirror, such was her influence, although I thought it a bit strange. She would sometimes open the back door in case a thunderbolt came down the chimney and could exit by the open door. I often imagined that it would be up to me to show it where the door was.

"This way please thunderbolt. Turn left in the hallway, that's good, now through the kitchen and left here, straight on, take a right and there you are. Out you go, have a good trip. For many years I feared thunderstorms. Nevertheless, she was a source of great fun and in her later years she would talk non-stop. Once we said we would cover her head with the tablecloth, like they did to parrots to stop them talking. She laughed, she let us do it and was immediately silent then we crept out of the room. We soon went back and took it off and she continued just where she'd left off. She was a wonderful lady.

Gran

Church Choir Pauline

I began going to The Congregational Church in Pontefract, my Dad's church. I quite enjoyed it as it was the same denomination and worship pattern as Silcoates. But Dad said that with such a good singing voice I ought to be part of the parish church choir. I thought that was a very kind offer he made to release me to worship in the Anglican church. I believe David organised the audition and I was accepted. It took some time for me to adjust but I was readily accepted as I had a well-trained voice and I could read music. I felt special in my robes although I never mentioned it to anyone. Choir practices were on Tuesday and Friday evenings and it was a crime not to attend unless you were ill. Fridays were best as Gran always used to give me three pence for a bag of chips on the way home. I made countless friends and it was a happy period in my life.

Pontefract is full of snickets and ginnels: short cuts usually into town. I used them to go to choir practice any one of them would bring you out into the market place. There was a choice of about five but I always went down the one that passed the surgery because just past the snicket 'proper', there was a row of houses and each of their doorsteps were pumice-stoned around the edges. If I was lucky I could walk past Pauline who always seemed to be sitting on her doorstep and she had the most beautiful kneecaps I'd ever seen in my life and a smile like the sparkle of sunlight on the first cherry blossoms of spring.

House Next Door

The house next door to us in Pontefract was called the Haven. A name I thought to be a bit exaggerated in view of the fact that it was surrounded on one side by a very tall wall with bits of glass on top to prevent intruders and on our side by a very tall fence. It was a home for unmarried mothers. In those days if girls were unfortunate enough to find themselves in such a predicament it was considered wise to keep them isolated in a home such as this. However, Margaret and I used to peep at the babies in their prams and climb the fence and pull faces at them to try to make them laugh. We managed to have little chats with their mothers and made friends with them all. One day we were asked if we would like to go round to see some of the babies and we were delighted. Other visits followed and we made lots of friends and we became fond of a little boy called Richard and his mum. We even invited them to tea one day and they were allowed to come. For months we played with little Richard from The Haven and even walked out with his mum sometimes and she let us take turns to push the pram.

Soon it was time for his baptism and his mum asked us if we could go with her and little Richard as we were his best friends. We were really delighted to have this invite and Mum and Dad thought it a really nice thing to be doing. But come the day, Margaret was poorly and couldn't go.

"Margaret, I'm so sorry. We won't go."

"No, you go," she said, "and tell me all about it when you come home."

So, I put on my best blazer, clean white shirt, well-pressed grey flannel trousers and yellow socks and just checked myself out in a mirror.

"Good heavens," Dad said, "you look a bit smart, you'll startle the natives."

I set off for church on my own wondering what Dad meant about the natives as I didn't think any of them would be there.

I arrived just before three o'clock and sat near the font and said a little prayer for Richard as I thought that to be right and proper. I sat there with joyful expectation feeling very privileged and quite spiritual and as the baptismal party took their places I caught a glimpse of baby Richard. We sat there for a while in silence.

My peace was suddenly and deliberately shattered by a very firm grip on my shoulder and looking round the verger's face was right up to mine and in a hoarse and threatening manner he croaked in a loud whisper "Family only, out!"

My protests were in vain as I was forcibly manhandled out of the church door. Richard's mother was unable to protest either as she had little authority over the proceedings. It would have been quite different if she was married. That's the only time I've been thrown out of church and at the time I was bewildered and confused. Looking back the verger really stepped out of line and considered himself to have far more authority than he had.

I wonder if he would have thrown me out if on that day he realised he was throwing out a future Anglican priest.

As I walked home from the church back along the snicket I heard a voice like a tiny sanctus bell whispering deep within my soul. He never makes me welcome either Andrew.

And as I passed the row of houses Pauline was still sitting on her doorstep and she gave me one of her beguiling smiles and I thought I saw her blush ever so slightly and I felt at one with the world again.

Christmas Supper

Mum and Dad formed a special friendship with the Outwins who were farmers. Their farm was way up a hill past the park. It was quite some way to reach it and even if you caught the bus which stopped outside the farm there were two large fields to cross before you reached the farmhouse.

Mr Outwin looked like a typical farmer. He had a well-weathered face that bore the evidence of years of confrontation with the outside elements. His clothes seemed to be made up of several layers of brown checked woolly material and he wore a pair of well-worn stout leather boots. He was a well-built elderly man and he walked with a stoop. His head balanced a very worn flat cap that he kept pulling down over his forehead.

His wife was delicate and very polite and prim. She had quite a wardrobe including some long flowing cotton dresses which she wore during the daytime and seemed unusual for the time. But she always wore the same round brimmed hat. I grew to really enjoy their company especially when they called round unannounced on several occasions.

Mr Outwin used to take his farm produce around Pontefract on a cart pulled by a very docile horse called Bella, supplying his customers with fresh vegetables and he used to call at our house. One day Margaret and I were bored and we just happened to say to him,

"We wish we could have a ride on your cart."

"Ee, by gum, you can if you like, but you'll have to sit still mind, along 'back o'cart, no fallin' off like, heh." He had a young lad with him who wanted to be a farmer and he was always with the cart controlling Bella. His name was Tommy.

"We've got some passengers today Tommy. Tharl look after 'em wont the?"

"Ah will mister."

So off we went and from that day we always had the opportunity of riding on the cart. Sometimes we felt a bit self-conscious when we called at people we knew and they would say,

"Oh, it's you."

Tommy would often offer me the opportunity to hold Bella still by the reigns when we stopped. But after the first time I realised how big Bella was and I declined. The rides were a real experience. One thing we both didn't consider and perhaps we should have was that we were sitting behind a horse and quite often it suffered from uncontrollable flatulence!

Our friendship with the Outwin's grew and one winter's night we were all invited to the farm to have supper with them.

Christmas spirit was already in the air. The shops were festooned with all sorts of gifts and toys and Christmas decorations and we had already put up our Christmas tree and streamers and our house was full of Christmas cards from all our friends and relations.

It was already dark as we set off for the farm. Margaret my dearest sister had made a Christmas posy for Mrs Outwin and Mum had made a few mince pies which she carried in a tin box.

Mr Outwin met us at the gate to the farm yard. He was dressed in a very smart tweed suit and a red tie and he looked so different, apart from the fact that he still wore his old battered and well-worn cap perched on his head.

"Come on," he said, "t'missus is inside."

As we picked our way through the darkness I saw to the right of the yard a huge barn that was stacked high with hay and had all sorts of odd looking machinery scattered around it. On the left was a tiny gate that looked as if it lead to the main yard and we could hear the soft lowing of cattle from the sheds and the smell of hay that always seemed to spread its scent over all farm yards.

I wondered if this was a bit like the farm yard in which Jesus had been born. I bet it isn't far off.

The sudden brightness from the kerosene lamp as we entered the farmhouse after the blackness of the outside made our eyes squint. The inside of the farm house was bright and cosy and very welcoming. Mrs Outwin made a real fuss of us all and in wishing us all a Happy Christmas offered some of her homemade gooseberry wine or a sherry. Most chose a sherry. I put my hand out but it was quickly withdrawn.

"It's not really for you lad," Dad said.

"We know what homemade wine can be like," said Mum. "It can make you a bit wobbly. Oh go on then. I'll try just a little drop seeing as how it's Christmas."

Whereupon a very large glass was put into her hand and as Mum smiled a big smile Dad was heard to whisper. "You be careful."

There were many joyful sounds as we entered the dining room not least because of the magnificent array of Christmassy treats that covered most of the table. The eye could hardly take it all in. There were sausage rolls, pork pies, a very large salmon decorated with cucumber, plates of vol-au-vents and a huge cooked ham, ready to be carved. There were mountains of mince pies, a three-tiered cake stand full of brightly coloured cakes and buns, a large bowl of trifle and to top it all a square iced cake wishing everyone a Happy Christmas. Such a sumptuous feast. I couldn't wait to tuck in.

"What a spread. What a treat. How generous. You must have been preparing this for days." Everyone was calling out at once.

"Oh it's nothing as long as we've enough to go round." said Mrs Outwin modestly, "Now before we sit down for supper I thought we would have a few games."

"O Lawd," I thought, "why can't we just sit down and tuck in?"

But we all joined in the usual favourites of eye spy, Charades, guess what I am thinking of, twenty questions and animal, vegetable or mineral, which was a popular radio programme of the day. Lots of fun and merriment after which we sat down at last to the supper of a lifetime. There was so much food that even when we could eat no more there was still sufficient left to provide another sumptuous feast.

Having fed well I let my now sleepy eyes have a good look around the room. It was old, traditional and had a worn and well used feel about it

Pictures of old farm buildings and families, long since gone, were hanging around the walls and there was a painting of a fox. The furniture and chairs were from a bygone age and next to the fire was a very large wooden rocking chair. In front of the brass fireguard was a rag rug. The fireplace was an old black leaded range and tonight the embers glowed. Red and hot the logs intermittently burst into flame and then died down changing the room's interior from a flickering light to a warm glow. I came out of my cosy slumber when I heard music from the piano.

Mrs. Outwin played the piano quite tunefully on an instrument that had seen better days and we sang carols. We seemed to sing a great many carols that night as everyone had a favourite. I was beginning to feel drowsy again but I suddenly heard Dad and Mr Outwin singing a duet. They were singing with great gusto and I wondered if they were imagining they were in the Albert Hall. I had never heard Dad sing like that before and I was taken aback.

After that it was time to go home and as we left the comfort of that magical farmhouse and stepped out into the farm yard it began to snow.

Picnic in the Park

Dad loved his books and he liked to tell Margaret and I stories from them especially at bedtime. One of his favourites was The Wind in the Willows by Kenneth Graeme.

Once when he had been redecorating the house with Mum suddenly just like Mole, who we are told had been spring cleaning his little home, Dad flung down the brush on the floor said "Bother!" and "O blow!" and also, "hang spring cleaning!" and would have bolted out of the house without even waiting to put on his coat, had it not been for Mum crying out "What's the matter with you?"

Dad could often appear to be quite strange and was capable of the bizarre. He often walked around with a teapot cosy on his head and sang silly ditties to himself. Such as:

"Find a donkey, find a donkey, stroke its head and pull its tail."

"I've told you before and I'll tell you again, don't pull the feathers on my little black hen."

And

"Shan't I be glad to be bloomin' well dead!"

This last one used to upset my mum and every time she caught him singing it she told him to hush and stop being daft.

Looking back on those days of my childhood it was good to have a Dad who was a bit different, but my life was helped by a Mum who was stable and a Gran who was the kind of person who was always there as a listening and supportive backup.

It was a good spring that year. The year the decorating was done and there was quite a joyful atmosphere in our house. The days were sunny and it was good to be outside in the freshness of the air. The cherry blossom tree was beginning to flower and buttercups and daisies were pushing up on the lawn. Dad was a keen gardener and he was pleased that the seeds he had sown were beginning to show signs of life.

Gran had decided to go on a visit to Aunt Clara in Brimington so Mum was on her own and seemed to spend a lot of her time reading her favourite magazine, "The People's Friend". She always read me the stories that appeared every week about a little robin.

Then one morning at breakfast Dad made one of his profound announcements.

"I think today we'll take a picnic to the park and go on the lake on one of the rowing boats."

"That'll be really nice," we all said.

"Nice?" said Dad. "It's the only thing" and he went on to quote from one of his favourite authors. "Believe me, there is nothing – absolutely nothing half so much worth doing as simply messing about in boats. Simply messing about."

At that point in time we all agreed with him and became really excited at the prospect of messing about on the lake.

From then on it was another picnic packing session but we managed to limit the carrying to just two bags and having sorted it all out we set off on our adventure to the lake. The park was not far away and we were soon walking up the wide drive that lead to the main gates.

The picnic was soon consumed. We sat on a grassy bank quite near to the lake and Margaret was once again chief sandwich passer. But I was more interested in the boats and I couldn't see them from where we were sitting. I wanted to know what they looked like and if they were big or small.

David looked as if he was about to nod off and so I gave him a prod. How could he be so sleepy at such a critical point in the afternoon.

"Come on let's go then," said Dad and off we went along the path and along the lakeside to where the boats were moored.

"I think we'll need a big one to get us all in." I said.

The boatman agreed with me and he pulled a brightly coloured large rowing boat alongside.

"Who's rowing?" he asked.

"You'd better row," said Mum to Dad and we all agreed.

"Tell you what," Dad said, "I'll go round the lake and then you can all have a go."

"That's a good idea. Can I be first?" I asked.

"No, David can be first because he's the eldest and in any case he's been rowing before."

So we all helped each other aboard and found a seat. The boatman had a long pole and pushed us off and it felt like we were surrounded by dark and threatening water as we pulled away at a steady pace.

"Keep an eye on those swans," Mum warned. "They look as though they're coming over here and I've heard their beaks can break your arm or your leg."

"You'll be alright," said Margaret, "they won't hurt you."

But nevertheless I kept a beady eye on them.

Soon we were well up the lake and praising David on his performance.

The sun was up now and it cast warm violet shadows across the banks of the lake as the water between rippled with grey dappled light. Dragonflies hovered above the water lilies and a water rat appeared from nowhere alongside our boat.

"Look Dad, there's Ratty out for a swim, looking for mole,"

"Why so it is, fancy seeing him here."

"I think he came to say "hello."

Dad could always go along with a make believe and sometimes I wondered if he really was part of another world, because often he didn't seem part of this one. David completed very commendable rowing. He hardly splashed us at all.

When it was my turn everyone started to make a fuss.

"Do be careful. No, put both oars in at once. Go straight. Go straight. You've wet me through. Sit in the middle. For heaven's sake watch what you're doing." Everyone was suddenly calling at the same time.

"Leave him," said Dad, "and let him learn for himself it's the only way."

I wasn't doing very well but I was doing my best and I was really enjoying this. For the first time in my life I felt responsible for the safety and welfare of all my family.

"Look ahead! Stop!" cried the voices in harmonious panic.

But it was too late.

Our boat struck the bank of the island in the middle of the lake with some speed. I could see from my rowing position that everyone had managed to grip their seats and slide forward graciously. Mum was behind me at the front of the boat and looking around I swiftly turned back and averted my eyes for she had slipped from her seat and was lying on her back on the floor of the boat with her legs up on the air exposing what no one should see, especially me!

"You idiot!" called David. "Didn't you see what was about to happen?"

"How could I? I was facing the other way."

Anyway I was man enough to say sorry for what I'd done and at least I'd learnt another lesson. Look behind when you are rowing. In later life I found this useful advice for all manner of situations.

On the way home Dad thought the afternoon had been great and a good time had been had by all. Mum's legs in the air incident was the climax of the day and we all thanked her for being such a good sport.

Walking back home dad did one of his silly walks and said, "there's nothing half so much worth doing as simply messing about in boats."

Mum said, "There is!"

Mum

A New Brother

It was shortly after that I began to notice something strange about Mum. She seemed to be putting on a considerable amount of weight and she was always hungry. Every day she appeared to get bigger and she had to rest quite a lot. I just thought to myself that if I was getting as fat as that I'd have to sit down and rest most of the time as well. I hadn't a clue what was going on until one breakfast time when we were all together Gran said "Well, aren't you going to tell them all, our Elsie."

By then I think I had a fair idea.

"Well," Mum said, "I'm going to have another baby."

"Wow! Wow! Wow!"

Everyone seemed to have known about all this for some time before I'd begun to sort it all out for myself. No wonder she was getting so big! What a relief I thought, at least she'll get back to her normal size when it's all over. It would have been awful if Mum had stayed as big as she was now forever.

It really was fantastic news. "What are you having Mum? A boy or a girl?"

Margaret said, "Don't know that, till baby is born, no one does, that's why Mum has been getting ready for either. What would you like, a boy or a girl, sister or brother?"

"I don't mind," I said, "I'm just looking forward to having a new baby."

But then everyone seemed to be looking at me rather quizzically.

"Will it matter to you Andrew if you're no longer the youngest of the family? You'll be knocked off your perch of being the youngest. You won't mind will you?"

"Don't be daft," I said, "that never crossed my mind. I'm so looking forward to it all."

But then I thought "I hope it's not going to make a difference to me, I hope I'll still be treated the same."

Time came and went and so did the midwife who seemed to be a constant visitor to our house. So much so that I became a good friend and when she bought the latest car on the market, a Morris Minor, she asked me if I'd like to accompany her on her rounds and have a ride in it, as I'd admired it so much when it was parked outside our house on her visits. We spent a lovely morning together and I promised that I'd help her to deliver baby if she needed me. She rapidly declined my offer and when the great day arrived my sister and I spent hours waiting on the stairs until we heard the first timid cries of a new born infant. It was a boy! On first seeing him he looked a bit wrinkled and tiny and it was surprising how much noise could be created from something so small.

Margaret, David & Andrew

Railway Cottage

We always went on a summer holiday when we were children and one of our favourite places seemed to be Filey. I think Dad must have liked it because he seemed to book somewhere there each summer. On one occasion he had this bright idea of hiring this ex-railway carriage situated on a caravan site.

We'd previously rented rail carriages owned by the railways that were converted into holiday homes. These were shunted up sidings in quiet areas of the countryside and were very comfortable and spacious.

"We all like it at Filey," said Dad, "so let's give it a try." And so we did!

When we arrived at the caravan site we saw lots of beautiful and attractive mobile homes and we were full of anticipation as we sought out our rail carriage.

"O lawd," I said as it came into sight.

"O lawd," everyone said as they all spotted it.

"Come on," said Mum, "let's open up and take a look inside."

The carriage from the outside looked as though it had been simply dumped where it stood, in its original state. Paint was peeling off the sides and the windows were dirty. It was coloured brown and black but showed signs of years of fading. Inside the original cautions and warnings were still in place.

"Do not lean out of the window".

"Do not pull the stop cord except in an emergency".

"Do not use this lavatory when the train is standing at a station".

"O Lawd," I said again, "Does that mean I can't have a wee for a fortnight?"

At least Gran laughed.

We soon got used to our new surroundings and had a wonderful time in Filey. The cobbled landing and the fishing boats are still there today and so is Corrigans the amusement arcade, the joy of my life when I was young. In those days there was a ball bearing that you could shoot around a circular ring and if you could get it into certain slots a cigarette would fall out at the base of the machine. I always found this a great temptation and had many secret smokes on my winnings.

The railway carriage was a bit short of space at bed time. There were four bunk beds in the first section, two along each side of the carriage. I had to sleep above Gran because otherwise we couldn't have fitted her in. Fortunately, I was on the top bunk but it had its disadvantages. My nose was perilously near the gas lamp.

There was no electric and although the gas lamps and oil lamps gave a very warm and attractive light you had to make sure they were all out at night.

"Well, that's great," I said, "it looks as if I shall be gassed in my sleep. Ta very much!"

"Oh shut up and stop making a fuss"!

The night progressed and all became peaceful. It was early morning when Gran gave a mighty scream.

Everyone came rushing to her aid.

"What on earth's the matter, mother?"

"What is it? What is it?"

"What a fright," she said, "what a fright," she was still trembling.

"It was our Andrew."

Oh, here we go again. What have I done now?

"When I woke up, Andrew's arm was hanging out over his bunk and it was right in front of my face. It gave me such a fright. I thought it was a ghost or something, come to strangle me."

"Stupid woman," I said under my breath.

"I heard that," said Mum, "don't be saying things like that about your Gran!"

Everyone made a bit of a fuss of her and I just lay there thinking, never mind my arm, I'm just glad the rest of me wasn't gassed in the night.

An Unusual Fairy

Later in life when I had two children, both girls, I thought it would be nice to revisit Filey and recall the earlier holidays we spent there in my childhood. So my wife Jenny and myself, on the recommendation of a friend, booked into a bed and breakfast on the cliff top.

We were greeted by an elderly lady who was dressed in the sort of outfit that would suit a fortune teller at a fairground.

"Welcome my dears, welcome to my abode here in Filey. It's really nice to meet you."

From the hallway we were shown into the dining room.

"This is where I serve breakfast in the morning," she said.

The dining room was pink. Everything was pink. Pink table cloth on the table, pink chairs, pink curtains, pink carpet, every single item in the room was pink, including the artificial plastic roses in the bay window. To crown it all in the middle of the mantelpiece was a plastic fairy with a pink light up her bottom.

"You can see that I like pink," she said.

That night when we went to bed we had to fight with the mattress. It forced us into the middle of the bed and the edges curled up and kept slapping us in the face. The only way to get any sleep was to lie on the edge of the bed to keep the mattress flat.

The breakfasts were massive and over generous which made the holiday for me.

When I asked the children what they liked best about the holiday, without doubt they both agreed that it was "the fairy with a light up her bum!"

Seahouses Funeral

When I was appointed to my first headship, I always tried to offer some new experiences to the children. I made provision for the older Junior School children to spend some time together on a holiday of educational experience as well as relaxation, usually towards the end of the summer term, before they progressed up to senior school.

On one such excursion we stayed at a cheery hotel in Seahouses. When we arrived we were informed that the chef had done a bunk and the young owners were struggling with the food preparation. As a result, the food was really quite abysmal. However, the children were very cheerful about all this and kept a brave face.

The problem with the meal situation reached its climax when my Deputy Head complained that when she'd tried to cut into her sausage it rose up at both ends, the bread buns cut her tongue and her morning tea she said was not Lyons Brew but cats!

"I think," she said, "we ought to do something to show our children that we care."

I thought quickly and so at breakfast I told the children to gather all the food they couldn't eat and put it in the carrier bag I had given to my trusty deputy, Mrs Bowness.

In the meantime I made a makeshift coffin from some cardboard boxes I'd found around the back of the hotel and managed to gather all the children to the front of the hotel. The food was placed in the coffin and I told the children that as we'd all had enough of it we would go and bury it at sea.

The coffin was carried by four of the older girls and the rest of the party walked in solemn procession behind. One or two really joined in this extraordinary ritual by singing a bit of "Abide with Me". What a sight we made as we meandered down through the streets of Seahouses.

People stopped and cars slowed down.

"What's happening. What are you all doing?"

"It's a funeral, we're burying dead food. We're going to bury it at sea."

In the meantime, I was quoting from the funeral service as we wandered on and we gathered quite a crowd. Eventually we reached the shore line and the edge of the sea.

"Right," I said, "just throw it all into the sea and let the gulls enjoy it."

As these lovely children who'd joined in this lark with such enthusiasm tossed in the remains, I just made up a few words to commit all this food to the mighty ocean. I remember the laughter of so many children some of whom were rolling about on the sand.

My deputy said, "They'll remember this for such a long time."

And they did.

"Mr. Woodhouse. Look there's no seagulls about. Them sausages must have killed 'em!"

We were lucky with the weather that year and as far as I remember the sun shone every day. Holy Island was a good place to explore and I thought the children would like to visit the small but delightful garden just below Lindisfarne Castle. So we set off in good spirits and when we arrived I tried to tell them something about why this little garden was so special. I gathered them together and told them about Gertrude Jekyll the nineteenth century garden designer from London who'd designed this garden for Edward Hudson in 1911. He was the owner and publisher of the magazine Country Life.

"Me mam gets that!"

I went on to say that Gertrude was influenced by William Morris and John Ruskin. In some ways I wished I hadn't mentioned them as I was asked, "Who?"

After searching my mind to recall these famous artists and their achievements, I felt as though I was getting off track and the children were getting restless, so I just finished by saying that Jekyll used an existing walled enclosure (probably a vegetable garden) to make this flower garden and put in a decorative sundial.

"What's a sundial, Sir?"

"It's over here," I said, "come and see for yourselves."

I did my best to show them how the shadow from the sun made a kind of clock.

"Heh, its bigger than your watch, ha, ha, ha."

"Off you go then and enjoy the garden."

And so we all did, including staff and helpers.

"My Dad says the devil lives in our garden cause 'nowt grows. He took to growing vegetables until our Mary, me little sister picked all the flowers on his green beans and gave 'em to me Mam!" said Billy Watson afterwards on our way up to the castle.

"That's a shame," I said.

But I must admit he'd made me smile.

As it was a very hot day we thought we would have a trek around the island. We decided to go across the middle instead of the shore and see what was there. First though I lined all the children up in a crocodile formation, a long line in pairs so we could keep them all in view. Some of the helpers were in the middle section and Mrs Bowness my deputy brought up the rear. So we set off.

I hadn't reckoned to take into account the terns! Apparently it was their nesting season and they just didn't seem to like us.

"Keep your heads down children and cover your heads with something if you can."

It was then that it all happened. A tern flew low over the rear of our procession, swooped all along the line missing everyone, but it landed on my head with its very sharp bill and took a great big peck at my exposed head.

Immediately, Janet Walker who was just behind me, turned around and shot her hand high into the air and bellowed, "Mrs Bowness, Mrs Bowness, Mr Woodhouse swears!"

Vandalised Garden

Dad was a keen gardener and although our garden behind the house in Pontefract was not very large he kept it in good order and cultivated some lovely flowers in it. Towards the back of the garden on the edge of the lawn stood a cherry blossom tree and beyond that he grew vegetables. For some reason the large and solid blue gate set in the wall at the rear of the garden didn't shut. All it needed was a slight adjustment but no one seemed to bother and it was held shut by dragging a huge block of concrete behind it. We had to negotiate this every time we left the house by the gate.

I was often the errand boy who was sent out to the two shops on the corner across the road. One was a general store and the other a family butcher. I was often sent to the store for some sugar and in those days it was shovelled out from a large tub into a bag made of thick blue paper. All goods like sugar, salt, currants and raisins and even tea were kept in containers and scooped out to be weighed on a pair of scales kept for this purpose on the well-polished mahogany counter. The goods were counter balanced by brass weights ranging from half an ounce upwards. Sweets were weighed in the same way and we used to count how many we got for two ounces and usually chose the smaller sweets for best value.

But I always liked going to the butchers best of all. Meat was still on ration and we had to buy cheaper cuts to make the meat ration last. Gran was a brilliant cook and introduced us to sheep's brains on toast, that I simply adored. They were like tripe with lamb flavour. But the best of all was pig's head. Gran could make this into a gourmet meal. She picked out all the best bits and it was simply delicious. So I enjoyed being sent to the butchers for these.

When I opened his door he always said, "Oh, It's you again!"

But I enjoyed going for a different reason than collecting meat. It gave me the chance to say, "Me Gran wants to know if you have sheep's brains and a pig's head?"

Going back home I always had to struggle with the back gate and would put the brains and the pig's head on the floor in the butcher's bag whilst I closed it. Every time the pig's head seemed to be smiling as it looked up at me from the bag.

One day returning from a day out we found that our garden at the back of the house had been vandalised. The plants were broken and the vegetables trampled on. We were all shocked to see this and felt really sorry for Dad who treated his garden as his pride and joy. We could only guess that whoever had done this had climbed over the garden wall. There seemed little we could do except give Dad a hand over the next few days to tidy up and re-plant. Dad informed the police who came on a visit but there was little they could do except keep watch for a while. I remember Dad getting a bit agitated when they wanted to know his age.

"My age," he said, "my age?" "How will that help to catch them?" and he refused to let them know how old he was.

"But you see Dad" I said to him, "perhaps they were thinking it was an inside job."

But he was not amused.

Some strange happenings went on in our garden after that. Planks of wood were delivered and roofing felt and rolls of wire netting appeared and a couple of feeding troughs.

"What's happening Dad? Are you opening kennels?"

"It's a secret my boy. You'll have to wait and see."

It wasn't long before a hen house was erected and painted.

"In future we'll have fresh eggs every day and we may even have a few to sell!"

So a few days later the tiniest chickens arrived from our farmer friend Mr Outwin and were shooed into their new house.

"Good heavens Dad they're a bit tiny aren't they?"

"No, they're bantams, not chickens and they lay lovely small eggs."

"Tell you what Dad, you ought to have bought a load of geese instead. They would've been able to guard the garden."

Dad didn't seem to find that funny, so I went over to the "bantam" house and waited for the first egg.

The Kiss

My days at Pontefract were full. I was always busy doing or planning. I remember the early morning dashes to catch the eight twenty-five bus to Wakefield and how some mornings I missed it and when I got to school I had to tell the little white lie that it was so full I couldn't get on. I enjoyed Wakefield Grammar School and made many friends. John Place was my best friend, we just seemed to get on well with each other. He was keen on model Hornby trains and so was I. We collected the wind-up versions of gauge O and we often spent our Saturday afternoons together at his house at Sandal just outside of Wakefield.

The school encouraged me in my strengths and although I wasn't keen on academic subjects I excelled in music and my dear friend Dr Saunders waited for me after lessons on Saturday mornings to give me a lift to the Cathedral where he gave me piano lessons. I had a Fine Art Master who recognised my talent and a skilled woodwork teacher who encouraged my woodworking interests and guided me into making a lovely raffia woven stool that I still possess. These were all non-academic subjects but served me well in later life and sowed the seeds of my artistic career.

My free time was taken up by the church of St Giles where I was a chorister. We had practices on Tuesday and Friday evenings as well as two services on a Sunday, Matins and Evensong. Any absence apart from illness from these commitments was badly frowned upon. I enjoyed the singing but have to admit I also enjoyed wearing the choir robes with the frill around the neck. When we wore a stole at Easter and Christmas I felt a strange emotional surge in my being and a kind of spiritual wholeness in my soul.

I soon had many friends at church from both the choir and the congregation. Boys and girls seemed to mix naturally together. This was such a contrast to life at the all-boys boarding school and it took me some time to adjust. However, I began to notice a girl who always sat at the end of the pew. She sat with her friends and we often used to meet up after church.

She always wore blue and it suited her. After a few of our get together's following church we became very close friends and had a friendship that lasted many years. Her name was Margaret Carter. I really became besotted with her and we often managed to have a quick hello when I was dashing for the bus to Wakefield.

One sunny afternoon we found ourselves together in the Valley Gardens. It was a beautiful place with flower beds covered in dahlias, petunias and chrysanthemums surrounded by neatly trimmed lawns that lined the pathways. We wandered around for what seemed ages, content with each other's company and just chatting about nothing in particular. I suddenly became aware that we were holding hands.

"Look at this," I said, "did you realise we were holding hands?"

"So?"

"Gosh! You've got such lovely hands."

"I know," she said. "Tell you what, just follow me and I'll take you down my hidden lane."

I followed her and wondered where she was going. It was a very narrow track that lead away from the gardens and after a while she stopped and turned around. She looked straight into my eyes and as I looked at her, my body melted into a dream.

"Kiss me," she said.

I didn't know how. But she did and as she took my head and pulled my face onto hers our lips met and engaged.

"Again," said Margaret and I took a deep breath. Never to be forgotten that first encounter with the sheer heat of love and the warm pink glow from her cheeks as we gave a final embrace. I'd kissed and been kissed. My soul felt as though I had tasted of the forbidden fruit and my mind was being caressed by a thousand angels.

We stayed a short time and on a park bench pledged our future loyalty to each other. Then made our way home.

That night when the daylight had faded and the darkness blocked out the day, I remembered Margaret and felt like I'd kissed an angel and had liked it.

After that my days and nights were enriched as Margaret Carter seemed to occupy both my waking moments and my dreams. We met as often as we could and my studies at school seemed to take second place. I'd come to realise that love could be a powerful force and so precious that I wanted to keep it to myself and for it to be my God given secret.

Our love for each other grew and I believe it would have become eternal if the direction of our lives had been different.

Dad had been away from home for a few days. He didn't say where he'd been, but when he came home it was late at night and Mum made a great fuss of him.

"It'll be some time until we hear anything," he said.

It was several days later that he announced that he'd been all the way to Dorset and he'd now received a letter inviting him to minister to three churches there, Cerne Abbas being the main one and he'd accepted.

Margaret Carter

Cerne Abbas

My first thought was of Margaret Carter. Was I to be separated from her forever by the miles and miles between Cerne Abbas and Pontefract?

We were to move there in about three months' time so that gave very little time for fond farewells. But I did my best and kept her as close as I was able in that short time. I also spent time with my friends, who strangely enough seemed to envy my imminent departure to the countryside of Dorset.

Dad had told us that as he was unable to drive we may have to think about bicycles as a means of transport and to our great surprise we came home one afternoon to see three gleaming new bicycles in the dining room still with their wrappings on.

Margaret and I were so excited to have a new cycle each. It was like a dream come true. I was only sorry that David my brother was not at home to see all this. He was now serving his National Service and posted in Germany. So he didn't need a bike. So having said all our goodbyes and remembering the words of my woodwork teacher who had told me "Your mum will be able to hang out the washing in clean fresh air in the country" I went to bed with a heavy heart as I thought of everyone I was leaving behind but I looked forward to returning to the country and being closer to nature.

My sister Margaret and I were with Gran again. In those days Mum and Dad went before and we followed. It was a very rickety old bus and it had taken us some time to find the bus station in Dorchester. We didn't have much luggage and so we seemed to make good progress from the railway station.

"Are you going to Cerne Abbas?" we asked.

"Ooo arr," was the reply and I asked Gran what the bus driver meant.

"Ooo arr," she said and had a bit of a giggle.

He said "Ooo arrr!"

"Yes," she said, "It means yes, he's going there. That's a bit of Dorset dialect."

"He's having a bit of fun with us," said Gran. "Don't worry everyone speaks just like you, Andrew, most of the time."

"Good heavens," I thought, "where are we going?"

Brown and worn uncomfortable seats, a smell of hot oil, dirty windows and a conductor who seemed to have such a limited vocabulary he could only manage "Ooo arr" when asked a question, I wondered if we were on our way to a primitive and maybe ancient way of country living.

The bus trundled on and leaving the main road lurched to a stop further along the route in a narrow country lane. We had stopped outside the smallest Public House in England or so it said on a sign along the front of the building. I managed to catch the name of the village as Godmanstone as we approached it.

On we travelled and the countryside looked so beautiful and green and there were many farms to be seen. At last we saw a sign at the side of the road. Cerne Abbas. We'd arrived and Mum was there to greet us.

A new life began that morning as I stood by the old iron gate in front of the large white house that was to be our new home. I fell in love with it and thought it was the most beautiful house so far.

Inside all the belongings of our previous home seemed to be scattered around. Cardboard boxes hid their contents so no one quite knew where things were stored and upturned furniture and chairs with their legs aloft made any sort of available place to sit impossible. We first needed to search the house and take in the rooms. All were full of boxes and ornaments; every room was cluttered. Where on earth did all these things come from. I didn't remember half of them being in our previous home. I saw glasses, cups, plates, a grandmother clock, lots of photos, two fire guards and the old black bakerlite wireless we'd kept since the war days. There were boxes of shoes, a wardrobe, wellingtons, an ironing board with an iron tied to it and several boxes of knives and forks, in fact too many to name.

"What's our Andrew doing now?" called Mum.

"Come and get this tea I've made."

A hot and steaming teapot was placed on top of a side table along with the cups and milk. It was a welcome sight. Mum had bought some scones, so we indulged ourselves adding ample amounts of butter and jam.

"Golly," I thought to myself "This is the very first tea time in our new home."

Mum had bought the scones. She was a great cook but not a very good baker. She preferred to leave all the baking to Gran. Her efforts at making a fruit cake were comical. They were always heavy and I often pretended I couldn't lift them from the table to pass them. Once she announced that she had decorated the top of the cake with strips of orange peel and one teatime displayed her achievement to us all.

"Good grief Mum, what are they? Girders?" Fortunately, she took it in good spirits.

Our house, Cerne Abbas

My Wonderful Bicycle

My bicycle and I became almost as one after our first venture out. I was proud of its appearance and cleaned it and added all kinds of extra useful attachments. I regarded it as my trusty steed, like Bucephalus was to Alexander, a charger that could carry me beyond, out and away as we travelled the lanes and tracks of the Cerne Abbas landscape together.

I purchased a loud horn and a speedo for the handle bars, two great carriers on each side of the back wheel and a drinking bottle in case I was thirsty on my travels. I'd bought a dynamo that I rigged up on the front wheel and converted into a front light, and another to light up a light at the rear. Then I decorated it with flags and bunting just to finish it off. In fact, there was so much clobber it was so heavy I could hardly move, it let alone ride it. But I did and found a new freedom now I had wheels.

My bicycle was the greatest gift because for the first time in my life I was able to get away out into the wild countryside and go wherever my spirit led me. I spent days gliding along between hedgerows that encroached upon narrow lanes and felt the odd branches whisk through my hair as I passed. Spring brought out the primroses and violets and the best scent of all was from the bluebells. I found the stream that ran its course through the village and followed it out into the fields and beyond and here I found a pond that it fed and I was once again transported back to those days at boarding school and the Speech Day I sang, "The Trout" by Schubert, for there beneath these wavelets I saw "a tiny trout at play".

It was there on the river bank that I introduced myself to all the buzzing creatures that hummed and darted across and along that water. The slender dragonfly hovered just above the sap green reeds and several pond beetles dived below the clear crystal water. I watched with fascination as the pond skaters performed on the surface. Dad had told me to look out especially for the pond skaters as they were one of his favourite insects. I think it was because he too loved to watch their antics on the water.

A Wet Bugle

Margaret and myself were transported to school by a coach that stopped in our village. Margaret soon settled into her new school, but I found mine quite a different regime to my previous one. Most of the teachers were a bit elderly and old fashioned.

The French teacher, it was rumoured, suffered from shell shock from the last war where he'd served in some sort of resistance. He also had a bit of a twitch. If anyone misbehaved he had them in after school for what he called "interrogation." He often called out a name as he was teaching and speaking in French.

"Truscott! Interrogation after school, my room four o'clock."

Once he really lost his temper and proceeded to put the offending pupil's satchel in the middle of the aisle between the desks, take a run up to it and kick it up to the ceiling. Such was the standard of teaching in those days. This same teacher in our 'O' level year decided he would only teach a handful of our form French, "as the rest of you don't have a cat in hells chance of passing," he said.

The English Master was very old and unsteady on his feet. He had a great urge to read from Sir Walter Scot's "Guy Mannering". I think this reflected his age and it truly bored the pants off us and his diaries of Addison and Steele did much the same, ensuring that it would take years to rekindle a real appreciation and love of literature.

I managed to retain my interest in art and painting, although there was no official art room. We had to work in a long Nissen hut that doubled up as a dining hall for school dinners. There was often an odour of cooked cabbage rather than the sweet smell of fresh oil paint!

195

The school had a Cadet force which we were all obliged to join. I quite enjoyed being a soldier on Wednesday afternoons and really got into the spirit of it all. I even rose to a Lance Corporal and gained my marksman badge for shooting.

My love of music inspired me to join the newly formed brass band. I had a bugle and practised hard, so much so that I became very efficient and was appointed leading bugler. We attended several parades but there was a very special occasion to come. Two sculptures had been carved for the new school gates and these were to be a memorial to the fallen in the last war. I was to play the last post and reveille. So practise I must.

Above Cerne Abbas is the Giant's Hill. On it there is a huge giant, its outline carved into the hillside and filled with chalk. I thought it would be a great idea to reach the top of the hill to practise on my bugle. I was out of breath after the climb so I took the opportunity to have a short rest and view the scene below. It was a clear day and I could see for miles. There was the village spread out below and I could make out the church and coffee shop and The Red Lion and there was the main road to Dorchester and all around me from left to right spread out the rolling distant hills and green fields. I watched as a herd of cows were being brought in across the fields for milking. I could just hear the call of the farmer as he encouraged his herd to keep going. I felt again the spirit of thankfulness that I was here in the midst of the peace of this place. So, having regained my breath, I blew on my bugle. I've never felt so exhilarated as I blasted out the reveille and it never sounded so loud and purposeful. This was the very place to blow it!

Suddenly angry shouts and curses drifted up on the tranquil air from below. I saw that the cows had scattered and were now running amock up the valley with the farmer hot in pursuit. As he ran he kept looking up at Giant's Hill.

Grasping my bugle tightly I ran over the brow of the hill as fast as I could and returned home by a different route firmly keeping my bugle hidden beneath my coat.

It was a pity that all this practise and preparation seemed to be in vain because when the great day arrived for me to perform in front of the memorial gates it rained heavily and my bugle mouthpiece got wet in spite of my efforts to protect it. The last post sounded good but the reveille suffered from several damp notes.

The Fight

My life in the village was quite peaceful and unhurried. I was content to roam the lanes on my bike and take in whatever the day had in store. I made a very special friend at school, Peter. His father was a woodwork teacher and he was building a small boat that could be floated on the sea at Weymouth harbour. It was an exciting project and I often cycled over to his home at Minterne Magna to share an afternoon with him and watch his Dad making his boat.

"When I've finished it," he said, "I'm hoping to buy a small outboard motor to power it. Then we'll take it over to Weymouth and launch it. You and Peter will be able to take it out on your own as long as you stay in the harbour."

Peter also had a small motor bike and we often raced it around his garden. They were good days and we spent a great deal of time together on the motor bike and eventually in the harbour on the new boat.

My peaceful existence was interrupted one day at school when I clashed with the school bully, who also happened to live in our village.

One lunchtime I was standing in the queue for the mid-day meal when suddenly Bill Fox came up to me and started pushing in front of me and tried to trip me up. After a while I'd had enough of that and punched him hard on his chest and shouted,

"Get off!"

"And if I don't?"

"I'll make you!"

He didn't and I did, and there followed a fight to out match any seen at White City.

I was cheered on by all the crowd that had formed a circle around us. I punched him as hard as I could because I knew I had to beat him to make him back off me for good.

Eventually we were pulled apart by a teacher and resumed our places in the queue. Bill stood there red faced and sporting two black and swollen eyes. I was pleased.

"Well done Andrew," echoed from many, many voices.

"About time he was taught a lesson."

Sadly, however my bottom lip was bleeding and I had to attend the hospital outpatients to have a stitch put in it. My Art Master took me and asked what had happened. When I told him he seemed to sympathise with what I'd done and strangely enough there was no more mention of it and no reprimand issued.

There was a very happy outcome to all this because the nurse at the hospital told me she was called Jill and was the vicar's daughter. So I made a new friend and through her I went along to the church choir practises on Friday evenings and our friendship blossomed.

I had a very strong tenor voice and so when the church choir were practising to sing, "The Crucifixion" by Stainer I was invited to take all the tenor solos. How I loved the music of "King Ever Glorious" and I sang my heart out. After the performance the choir were invited back to the Vicarage for drinks and supper and I was closely accompanied by Jill who told me on the way there that everyone had been moved by my singing and that I should be proud of my achievements. I wanted to kiss her for that but thought better of it. Perhaps later.

I met her in Dorchester at the bus stop one afternoon. We were both waiting for the bus back home to Cerne and realised that there was an hour to wait for the next one. "That's a long time to wait," I said. "I think I'm going to hitch a lift, it may be better than waiting."

"What do you mean?" she asked.

I explained to her that I'd walk out along the Sherbourn Road and then stick out my thumb and see if anyone would stop and give me a lift. I'd often done this before and had always been picked up.

"So I think that's what I'll do. Come with me if you like it's quite good fun and we can stick together."

"Let's do it then," she said and so we set off and wandered slowly along the main road. Several cars passed us by and we were just about to find the next bus stop when up pulled a tractor and trailer.

"Oi, you two. Where you going?"

"Cerne Abbas!"

"So am I, 'op on t'back!"

As beggers can't be choosers, we did and sat at the back with our legs dangling over the side. We couldn't stop laughing as cars passed us by and waved.

And so we trugged along at about twelve miles an hour, but I was happy spending all this time travelling with Jill. When eventually we reached the village, I noticed a few lace curtains pulled aside peeping at the sight of the vicar's daughter on a farm cart, with a young man.

A Chapel Organ

As a family we attended Sunday worship at the chapel. I had to go there as my Dad was in charge and it was only right that we should all support him. It was very different to the church surroundings I'd left behind in Pontefract. The chapel was quite small but was very well kept by the caretaker who lived next door to the Manse and shared some of the garden behind our house. Rumour had it that they had an outside midin and he used to use more than horse manure to fertilise his vegetables. Any produce he brought around to our back door was always accepted and then disposed of quickly. I must say his marrows and cucumbers were enormous. At harvest time his crops always took pride of place at the communion rail and were eagerly bought by unsuspecting bidders at the harvest supper auction.

Chapel became quite central to my life. The elderly lady organist who had played the hymns for decades decided to retire and there was no one to replace her. My mum thought it would be good if I helped out for a while as I could play the piano.

"It would only be for a short time," she said, "and in any case it would give you another interest and you know you'd like it. You might even get some little reward for your efforts."

My ears pricked up. A little reward? That's better!

So I took the role on and faithfully played the organ at Cerne Abbas chapel for years. I progressed slowly at first finding the pedals difficult. But I kept going and eventually Dad arranged organ lessons for me in Dorchester that I attended after school every Wednesday. It was through my organ teacher that I became a member of The Casterbridge Singers. He was the conductor and seemed pleased that I'd joined them. As this was also held on a Wednesday evening, it fitted in with the organ lessons. There was no hope of catching a bus back to Cerne Abbas at that time of night and so once again I relied on my trusty steed and peddled my way home lighting up the road ahead with my ever bright lamp.

I enjoyed village life and made several friends. On Friday evenings country dance lessons were held in the Village Hall. The lady teacher was very enthusiastic and Margaret and I loved to dance and had lots of fun on these nights. Elizabeth Roberts was a friend of my sister and had the largest brown eyes I'd ever seen. She was a superb dancer and her do-si-dos were executed with perfection. I always hoped to dance with her and even if we didn't start off as a pair, due to the nature of the dances, she would pass my way soon enough with the swing of the circle.

"Do you like my friend Elizabeth?" asked my sister on the way home.

"She's alright," I said.

During the summer holidays Elizabeth's Dad, who had a large farm on the outskirts of the village stopped me on my bike one day and asked me if I'd like to help out on the farm as his pig man had taken ill and would be away for some time.

So it was, that throughout most of that summer holiday I rose with the skylark and off I went on my bike to the piggery to clean out their pig sties and let them out into the daylight. When I opened the doors that had been closed all night there was a great rush of foul pig smells and fierce grunts.

Chapel Organ, Cerne Abbas

The Friary

Winter passed and the first new shoots of spring heralded the promise of new life. Snowdrops and winter roses were the first to show their heads whilst crocus and daffodils were racing to grow and form their magical flower heads.

I had more or less exhausted my cycle routes around and beyond the village and decided to explore further afield. I'd heard that somewhere near to Cerne Abbas there was a monastery and I thought it might be worth a ride over to see the monks and say hello. I'd no idea how to find them and so I called in the Post Office and asked the lady behind the counter if she could help me in my quest. She was renowned for knowing all the goings on in the village as she was obviously privy to her customer's conversations and gathered much information.

"Well, first of all," she said, "it isn't a monastery. It's a friary. There ain't no monks, just friars, although it's hard to tell the difference. But them friars up there wear brown wrap-around sort of cassocks like the black ones the choir wear in church. But as I say they're brown. As far as I know there's two sorts of buildings up there. One to house bad lads and t'other to house all the friars. Now remember it's a friary not a monastery. Have you any idea why it's called a friary and not a monastery?"

"Is it because it has something to do with Saint Francis," I proffered.

"Well done," she said," I think he had a lot to do with it. Anyway what you asking all this for?"

"Well I thought I'd have a ride over on my bike and see them."

"Good heavens," she said, "well the best of luck. Mind they don't keep you and put you in with the naughty boys."

With that she started to giggle at her silly suggestion, walked away and disappeared into her back room.

A few days after that encounter I set off to find the friars. I knew by now that the friary was situated at Hillfield but first I must make my way to Batcombe. I found these places on a map which I took with me in my back trouser pocket just in case I got lost en-route. It didn't take long to reach Batcombe, it was a really straggling village set in a valley with easy pedaling into the village but an effort to climb up the road on the other side. I later found out that on the summit of the hill above the village is a mystic stone called the Cross in Hand which is mentioned in Thomas Hardy's "Tess of the d'Urbervilles". Apparently it was the site where a terrible murder took place.

I very carefully ventured down the precipitous Batcombe Hill along a narrow lane which descended in the manner of what seemed to be a helter-skelter ride. I reached the bottom and found myself in front of a twelve-foot wooden crucifix. Here then was the entrance of The Friary of St Francis.

I parked my bike up against a tree and ventured in. Some people were working in the gardens and as I approached they looked up and asked me if I needed help. I told them that I had ridden over on my bike from Cerne Abbas and that I was just visiting the friary. I asked if it would be possible for me to meet any of the friars and just say hello. Several of the friars came over to welcome me and say what a pleasure it was to meet someone who was keen enough to bike over to just say hello.

I felt the journey had been well worth it and that afternoon I made some new friends. Before I left I invited them to call in to see the rest of our family if they were ever passing by Cerne Abbas, and if so stay for tea. When I arrived back home I told mum about my visit to the friary. She seemed to be very interested in my exploits until I mentioned "calling in for tea."

"What am I supposed to do if they all turn up? I won't be able to feed them all!"

One or two did call in but most turned down the idea of tea as they had to walk back to the friary and it was quite a long way. In any case tea would be waiting for them there.

I became particularly fond of Brother Nicholas. He called at our house quite frequently. Mum and Dad thought he was a bit special as well and looked forward to his visits. I would call on the friary often and had many pleasant hours on sunny afternoons in the gardens talking away to the friars and anyone else who might be there.

I noticed that Brother Nicholas' visits became very frequent and that my sister Margaret could quite often be seen sitting in our garden chatting away to him. I then began to notice that Brother Nicholas didn't visit as often when Margaret was away at teacher training college but strangely enough his visits increased when Margaret was home. He'd told me once that he hadn't taken his final vows.

Then suddenly one day he told us all that he was leaving the friary and was looking for new horizons. He was looking for a job and his name would revert to his christian name of Robert. This was all very sudden. But he had become very fond of Margaret and their love for each other had blossomed.

His future was uncertain and I think Dad was a bit concerned. Having taken various jobs including working on a farm and as a gamekeeper he decided to train for the ministry at Rochester and became a priest in the Church of England. Margaret waited for him and they were eventually married in the parish church of St Peter in Belper, Derbyshire in nineteen sixty. I had the privilege of playing the organ for the service.

Bob & Margaret on their wedding day

The Haybarn Fire

I could smell the smoke before I could see where it was coming from. As usual I was on my bicycle just roaming about and I was slowly making my way down the hilly road that lead to the village. It was a hot day and the corn in the fields was nearly ripe and ready for the harvesters. It was a beautiful sight and that's why I came down the hill slowly so I could take in the view and sniff the smell of the ripening corn that drifted across the lane. But now I could smell smoke and so I sped quickly into the village to see where it was coming from. It looked as though the cow barn at the Abbey farm had caught fire. I could see that there were cows inside and a farm worker was trying to shoo them out. There didn't seem to be anybody else about so I wondered how could I help?

I suddenly remembered that just across the lane from the farm lived two old ladies and I'd often seen their gardener watering their garden with a hosepipe. In fact, I knew where they stored it in the greenhouse. Abandoning my bike, I ran swiftly to their door and banged the door knocker as hard as I could. There was no reply, so taking things into my own hands, I rushed along the lane to a gap in their wall, leaped over and flew around their garden to the greenhouse and grabbed the hosepipe.

When I returned to the burning barn a few villagers had gathered by the barnyard gate. I quickly unwound the hose, connected it to a tap that was in the yard, turned it on and aimed it at the fire. I was proud of my efforts and I heard murmurs of "Well done lad" and "Great effort son" as the water from my hose formed a perfect parabola into the flames. But eventually it was too hot to stay there and I had to make a hasty retreat and reluctantly returned the hosepipe back to the greenhouse.

On returning I heard the bells of fire engines coming down the road. Sparks were now flying into the lane and had begun to dance perilously into the air. Some brushed along the surface of the lane like escaping fireworks and now yellow smoke puffed out vehemently from gaps in the brickwork. The cows had been rescued and they were now in the field at the back.

The firemen were very well built men in thick, dark blue uniforms and there was much shouting and noise and the fire engines revved to pump out their water tanks while some of the men raked the straw away from the fire. Smoke drifted across the village and formed a grey cloud above the houses and cottages. More men, women and children had come to watch and when the fire was eventually damped down and extinguished the firemen were given a round of applause.

After that someone shouted out, "What about Andrew? He was first on the scene with his hosepipe, I think we should say well done to him too."

So I also received a round of applause and I must say I was quite pleased.

I watched the firemen pack up and one of them asked me if I fancied being a fireman. I said that I wasn't too sure about that.

But I was sure, I didn't think it would be a career for me. In any case I didn't think I'd ever develop the muscles needed for the job.

I told the old ladies all about my adventure with their hosepipe and they said that I'd done right to take it and were fascinated with the story. When Dad got to hear about it he wasn't too pleased with me.

"You ought to think more," he said, "What you did was extremely dangerous and you might have been burnt or badly injured. What if something had exploded, where would you be then?"

Ah, well, you can't win them all and I expect he was right. I only tried to help, but next time I'd probably leave it to the experts.

The house in Cerne Abbas where the hose was borrowed for the fire

Village Life

I'd been given a hayfork, a shovel and a stiff brush as my pig cleaning out equipment. I wondered what the hay fork was for as I had a shovel. But it came in useful to lift the "pig wet" straw. I hadn't realised that some pigs especially the big fat ones could be very nasty tempered and looked for any opportunity to have a bite at my ankles. So, I approached every sty with caution and I used my hayfork like a trident and imagined myself as a gladiator in the Coliseum of Rome.

However, I was pleased to have a pair of substantial wellingtons on my feet for protection. I was happy when I had finished mucking out those pigs, leaving their sty clean for them. But I knew that they would foul them up again and I'd have to clean them all out once more the next day.

Mrs Roberts, the farmer's wife stopped my mother in the village street weeks afterwards and told her that her pigs had never been so well cared for or as clean since I was in charge. I was so proud and pleased with myself.

After cleaning out the pigs I was dispatched to the sledge. This was my favourite job on the farm. It was harvest time and the corn was being gathered in. The sledge was pulled behind the bailer which scooped up the straw lying on the field that was left behind by the thresher. It bound the straw into oblong bales and slid them onto my sledge. My job was to catch them and stack them on the sledge six at a time. Then I had to push hard and slide them off the back carefully onto the field to be collected later and put into barns. I really enjoyed this and it was so good to be out in the fresh air and be appreciated and encouraged by the other harvesters.

The summer days on the farm were full but there was also time to have moments of rest within the comfort of the straw. These were the times of taking in the scents and sounds of summer. Even now when I hear the buzz of frantic bees searching for pollen or the sight of hay stooks, I relive those days gone by. I recall watching the cabbage white butterflies in their scores and the sheer delight when Dad pointed out the red admiral. They were days of corn stubble scratched legs as we raced across the fields to chase a long-eared hare or even searching on our knees for a foolish field mouse who came out to look at the sun and quickly disappeared again. Our red faces were always aglow and the sun seemed to shine more often and felt hotter in those days. Life was good.

New Year's Eve

David came home for Christmas. He was now in training for ministry in The Church of England at Kelham. He thought Cerne Abbas was a very quiet village where nothing seemed to happen. Margaret and I told him about our country dance sessions but he wasn't really interested. He did come with us on the nights before Christmas though when we joined up with the church choir and villagers to sing carols outside most of the houses and farms in the village. I thought this was a wonderful thing to do and how we lifted our voices in "The first Noel" and "Hark the Herald Angels" although I thought sometimes that the angels were sounding a bit flat with all the exhaustion. Those nights were precious as we shuffled along in a fairly orderly fashion from place to place and bellowed out our musical Christmas greetings.

"Alright," said my brother, "what's it like on New Year's Eve then? Any dances, big celebrations, or happenings?"

"Nothing as far as we know," said Margaret and myself. "Have you got any bright ideas?"

He thought for a while then asked if the church bells were rung at midnight.

"We don't think so. Everybody seems to just go to bed."

"Well," he said, "I think they ought to and if no one is prepared to stay up and ring in the New Year then we shall do it ourselves."

"You must be joking. How on earth can we do that and get away with it without getting into real bother?"

"Listen," he said, "and I'll tell you."

We both listened intently to his plan and the more he told us, the greater was our enthusiasm to carry it out. So New Year's Eve afternoon saw the three of us go into St Mary's church, kneel down in a pew and pretend to be praying. When we were sure no one was about, we pushed open the door to the tower and climbed the spiral steps that led to the bell tower. Once inside we found the tiny door that opened onto the flat roof on the east side of the church and unlocked it, closing it carefully so that it looked perfectly shut as before. Then we quietly and carefully descended the tower steps and, peeping out of the bottom door to make sure no one was around, we nonchalantly sauntered out of the church and went home by way of the chapel. We went into the chapel and unlatched the window at the back of the schoolroom and made our way home.

We wrapped ourselves up in warm clothes and tiptoed towards the back door and tried to leave without being noticed.

"Where on earth are you lot going?" asked Dad, "Do you know it's nearly midnight? What are you all dressed up for? There's nothing happening this time of night!"

"We thought we would just pop out and wish a few of our friends a Happy New Year and leave them a lump of coal for good luck," David said.

Gosh, I thought to myself, that's fast thinking.

"Well don't be long then. Mum and I will wait up for you so make them quick visits!"

With that we shot out of the back door and into the night.

It was dark outside, very dark. We could hardly see our hands in front of our faces. We'd brought a torch but the battery was low and in its dismal beam we shuffled with faltering footsteps along the back streets to the beck that ran just behind the chapel. As we began to cross the rickety bridge over the stream a group of elderly men from the village were attempting to cross from the other side. They appeared to be the worse for drink and swayed from side to side, holding on to each other as they tried to keep upright.

David said, "O lawd, I hope they don't recognise us. Quick, look over the side of the bridge so they can't see our faces and pretend we're looking into the water as if we've lost something."

We followed his instructions.

As the men passed us by one called out, "Why look ya, it's them Parson's kids, gone daft. Tha wain't catch any fish this time o'night."

With that they all fell about laughing and two of them fell on the muddy bank.

We ran off and came up behind the back of the chapel and climbed over the low wall.

"Let's hope that window is still unlatched," I said. We pushed it open and in we climbed. There hanging along the wall at the back of the school room was a very long ladder which we removed and maneuvered out through the window.

Once outside, David took the front, Margaret, the middle and I carried it at the rear. Oh! What excitement we all felt.

This was a real adventure. Carefully we opened the chapel gates. These squeaked a bit as they were made of iron, but through we went and there was still no one about. We managed to carry the ladder all the way down to the church and propped it up against the roof at the back.

Putting it into position was hard work and we had to make sure it was upright so it didn't slip. Once in place David climbed up it first, then Margaret and I climbed close behind her to make sure she had her feet firmly on the rungs. Having reached the top, we crawled across the roof to the side door in the tower we had left open that afternoon and went inside.

"We made it. How about that!" said David. "Now let's pull on a bell rope. The Sexton's bell rope was the only one we could see. It would be far too dangerous to unleash all the bells and in any case we didn't know how. As we were about to pull on the rope the clock struck twelve.

"That's good timing," we all said.

When the clock had finished chiming we all gave great pulls on the single bell rope and we could hear the bell sound out our Happy New Year message to the citizens of Cerne Abbas.

"Right we'd better get going now before anyone comes to see what's going on," said David.

Carefully we closed the tower door and even more carefully we edged across the roof of the church to locate the top of the ladder. This was a difficult task but we eventually found it. Once we were on firm ground again we took up our positions on the ladder and transported it back, through the open window to its rightful place in the chapel.

Climbing back through the window, we closed it very carefully behind us and made our way back to the bridge over the beck, making sure there was no one in the lane, including the drunken gentlemen. We shuffled our way back home as the dark night enfolded us.

Dad was still up and asked if our friends had been pleased to see us at that time of night.

Oh, yes," we said, and with that we went to our beds tired but happy.

The next day we couldn't wait to see if anyone had heard the bells that night and what they made of it all. There were no reactions at all and apparently no one had noticed. I did hear one comment in the Post Office though. One of the elderly men we had met on the bridge that night was talking to the Postmaster.

"Do you know Fred, I could be almost as sure as I'm standing here, that I heard the church clock strike midnight twice last night".

"Tha needs to put more water with it Walter."

The chapel now "converted", at Cerne Abbas

Life in Belper

I scraped through my '0' levels and although I managed to gain seven of them they were not high marks and I was reminded of this several times by the new Master of the sixth form.

I could see that my progress, if any, in this sixth form was going to be arduous and uneventful. I was assigned three subjects for study; Politics, English Literature and Art. I had no interest in politics and expected to fall asleep in English Literature if we had the same teacher who droned on in a world of his own and was a fan of "Guy Mannering" by Walter Scott and Addison and Steele.

I was interested in painting but the Art room was consigned to a space at the end of the dining hall available only when the meal tables had been cleared.

Fortunately, I was rescued from the dilemma of having to spend another two years in this environment. I still had great ambitions for my life and although some of the Masters at this school may have been academics I found they bored the pants off me. But I was saved in the nick of time.

Dad said he had been offered a post in Belper in Derbyshire and we would move there before Christmas.

The new house was situated on top of a hill called the Laund. It was semi-detached and had a long garden at the back. I felt really at home there and just after Christmas visited The Strutt's School and met the Headmaster Mr Mathias. He was a very encouraging person and I was beginning to feel I was in safe hands. What is more he came to the Congregational Church where Dad was the minister.

This school had girls and boys and I felt rather strange on my first day. I was in the sixth form and I took Music, English Literature and Art, now in a proper Art room. I was so happy and was determined to work hard and get my 'A' levels.

I was the only boy in the arts sixth form, it seemed all the other boys were taking science subjects. I was in a class with twenty-six girls but I soon got used to it and made really good friends with them all.

I had three terms to study for my music exam and I knew that this would be hard going as I hadn't had the chance to take an 'O' level. Three of us were studying music and one of the girls called Christine helped me a lot. She was a good pianist and used to play the piano at lunchtimes and we became more than good friends. My music teacher said I had a good singing voice and Dad arranged for me to have singing lessons with a professor of music in Derby. I performed in Twelfth Night and sang the song "O mistress mine" and glanced at Christine as I sang it.

School was good and every day was a happy day. We had quite a glamorous English teacher, Miss Walker and she used to sit on a high stool as she extolled the virtues of Milton's "Paradise Lost". We were a bit naughty. There was a boy with whom I often shared a joke and he used to sit on the right of the class at the front and I on the left. When she was reading a passage he would put his hand high into the air and put it down again very quickly. Miss Walker would look up thinking someone was asking a question, then when she looked down again I'd do the same and she thought someone on my side was about to ask a question. We only did this occasionally and looking back I suspect she knew what was going on, but she was a good sport and probably realised that we naughty boys admired her tremendously. She got me through my English Literature and for that I shall always be grateful.

Saturday Job

I managed to get a Saturday job in a furniture store in the High Street. It was run by an old gentleman who was Treasurer at our church. The most popular items were kitchen cupboards that were portable and made in pastel shades and linoleum was in demand in all kinds of colours. This was used as a border around the room and then a carpet square was laid in the middle. Fitted carpets were not in vogue and I sold many carpet squares in various sizes. The carpets were laid flat on top of each other up on the second floor and it was my job to pull them back to display them to the customer. Most customers bought items on hire purchase. They paid a very small deposit and so much a week. It was my job to collect the payments as they brought them into the shop and enter their name, date and amount into a ledger book which we both had to sign. At the end of the day the manager had to tot up all the payments in the book and balance them with the cash. I was always surprised at the speed he could add up. Sometimes when the other male assistant was absent I was sent out to anyone who was behind in their payments and try to get money from them. I didn't enjoy this aspect of my employment as I sympathised with them and felt sorry for their embarrassment at being confronted by a very young person. I often failed in my mission.

One Christmas I had a job as an assistant in a record shop. This was really interesting and very busy. I sold lots of records. I remember the number one record that year was "Mary's boy child".

School was a great place to be and I enjoyed singing in the choir. My favourite piece was "Dance a Cachucha", from the Gondoliers. It had great rhythm and the girls tapped their feet and I liked that!

It was a well-disciplined school. We always began assembly with prayers and a hymn and at lunch time we said either an English or a Latin grace before meals.

My art flourished with lots of encouragement from the Art Master and he took the art group out sometimes at weekends to see exhibitions of established artists. My paintings were being appreciated by both pupils and staff and it was at this school a member of the staff said it was a pity I couldn't answer all my exams using a brush and paint. He suggested my paintings would see me through, with distinction.

A Policeman's Lot

There wasn't much entertainment in Belper. It had a cinema in the High Street and lots of Public Houses. The hill leading up from the town to The Laund where we lived was very steep and it seemed to take ages to reach the top. My middle aged gentleman friend who also worked in the furniture shop had to go home this way as well but he always slipped into the pub halfway up the hill to sustain himself.

"I'll have to just call in here for some refreshment," he used to say. "Do you fancy a pint? I'll buy you one. Come on, we'll just have a couple."

If he'd said that later on in my life, I'd have gladly joined him. But at the time I'd never tasted beer or had any alcohol and I didn't fancy any, so much to his surprise I declined.

The church had a very fine pipe organ and I was given permission to play it. Sometimes I managed to spend a whole afternoon in the holidays playing away and really making a great vibrant sound that echoed and re-echoed around the church. One afternoon I'd been hard at it and was in a great exuberant mood as I managed to play a very difficult piece loud and strong and without any mistakes. As I closed the organ I called out to the rafters, "Yes! Yes!"

Then I jumped upon my bike and let it free wheel down the hill into town. It gathered great speed. But here I was again, back in the country, music in my ears and the wind at my back. As I reached the main road at the bottom of the hill I slammed on my brakes and skidded left around a traffic light into the body of a great burly policeman.

"Oy, Oy, Oy! Stop! What's your game? What do you think you're doing?"

I stood there legs on either side of the cross bar.

I was going to tell him all about the joy I'd experienced just now on the organ but realised it would have no effect on the situation.

"Do you realise what you've just done?"

"I'm sorry officer, I ran into you by mistake."

"Yes, you most certainly did and if you'd been in a car I'd have you for dangerous and careless driving."

By now a small group of shoppers had gathered round and I wasn't sure who had their sympathies, me or the policeman.

"And," he went on, "do you know what this is?"

He got hold of the pole holding the traffic lights.

"They look like traffic lights to me and I'll tell you something else," he said. "They were on red and what does that mean?"

"Stop," I said.

"Exactly." He then began to take out his note book and write me out a ticket.

"Ahh, Oh dear," said the crowd.

"O heck," said I.

Then after he had completed his reprimand he let me on my way. I suppose he was in his rights to give me a ticket but I thought he was a bit mean. My notification of the fine arrived through the letter box a few days later. I was fined a pound, my wages for a Saturday in the shop. Gran felt sorry for me and said she would pay it. I was surprised to read of my crime in The Belper News later that week. My fame spread far and wide especially as I was the parson's son.

I was even more surprised to receive an anonymous letter through the letter box later that week containing a pound.

Holding Hands

I found that much of my time was taken up by school interests and singing. I'd never experienced a school that was so lively and full of encouragement. The school held a competition open to the sixth form only. It was concerned with the beauty of spoken English. Two set pieces were to be recited to the whole school and the judges. I was more or less pushed into entering by my girlfriends in the form I was in. I still remember the prose that was set.

The first was "Mending Wall" by Robert Frost. I even had a few elocution lessons to help me through it.

The other was a piece by Winston Churchill about his struggle with painting pictures.

On the afternoon of the competition all the readers were together in a classroom adjoining the hall. Most appeared to be quite apprehensive and a bit nervous and I tried to lighten the atmosphere. I endeavoured to make them laugh by saying the set pieces in a silly accent.

There was one of our English teachers by the door and another member of staff, who was in charge, came over to her and asked her if everything was alright.

"O yes," she said. "Andrew is calming all of his girlfriends!"

We were called out individually to make our presentation and I thought I made a fair effort. As it was I came second and was quite pleased.

I walked home with Christine who said some nice things about my performance and when we parted she gave me a big kiss. That in itself made it all very worthwhile.

Our friendship grew and she was very supportive and helped me with my music. Mum and Dad enjoyed her company as well. In the final year of school Dad bought me a new piano to encourage me and he purchased records of all the pieces of music I had to study.

I remember having to go to Sheffield with Christine and another friend of hers to sit the aural exam. We sat in the same room and each of the students were asked to play a cadence. They were all super pianists and each of them played on for ages in double quick time before hitting an impressive cadence to finish.

"O dear," I thought to myself here goes and I just played "Amen".

"That's fine," said the examiner, "that's a cadence."

We also had a sight reading to play, a bass to put to a melody and to sing a melody having been given the key chord.

Later he said that he was very impressed with my singing voice. I sang, "Rosen brach ich nachts" by Brahms and we discussed his works at length. Here I was on solid ground.

We left Sheffield by train and I seem to remember talking about the exam all the way home.

One of the works we had to study was "Theme by Thomas Tallis" by Vaughn Williams. It was built upon a hymn tune and I used to enjoy listening to it. Dad had bought this for me to help with my understanding for the exam. It was a good gift really, as I was able to remember the description and meaning of the music written on the record sleeve and include this in the written exam. I hoped it would be well accepted by the examiner.

I thought that part of the description on the record sleeve was spot on.

"This work is a musical version of a stained glass window".

I was pretty confident I'd pass my Art but not so sure about my English Literature. But there was no going back now and I certainly didn't wish to do so. The days arrived when the exams began and I just did my best.

Christine and I had become very close friends and we shared much time together. One day when I was working in the furniture shop Christine burst through the door.

"You've passed all three," she cried, "Yes all three. I've just been up to school and seen the list. Well done Andrew."

"Wow," I said, and dropping everything I dashed out of the shop and we both ran back to school. Sure enough there were the list of names including Christine and our friend Penny. The three of us had passed all our exams. We held hands and wished each other well for the future.